Conflict

D1149712

CONFLICT

Joyce Huggett

eagle

Guildford, Surrey

Copyright © 1998 Joyce Huggett

The right of Joyce Huggett to be identified as author of this work has been asserted by her in accordance with the Copyright, Design and Patents Act 1988.

Published in 1998 by Eagle, an imprint of Inter Publishing Service (IPS) Ltd, St Nicholas House, 14 The Mount, Guildford, Surrey GU2 5HN.

All rights reserved. No part of this publication may be reproduced or transmitted in any form or by any means, electronic or mechanical, including photocopying, recording or any information storage and retrieval system, without either prior permission in writing from the publisher or a licence permitting restricted copying.

In the United Kingdom such licences are issued by the Publishers Licensing Society Ltd, 90 Tottenham Court Road, London WIP 9HE.

All Scripture quotations, unless otherwise noted, are taken from the NIV, the *Holy Bible, New International Version*. Copyright © 1973, 1978, 1984 by International Bible Society. Used by permission of Hodder & Stoughton, a Division of Hodder Headline.

Other Scripture quotations are marked:
JB – *Jerusalem Bible*, © 1966, DLT.
GNB – *Good News Bible*, © 1966, 1971, 1976, American Bible Society.
LB – *Living Bible*, © 1971, Tyndale House.
The Message, © Eugene Peterson (NavPress).
NKJV – *New King James Version*, © 1982, Thomas Nelson Inc.
RSV – *Revised Standard Version* © 1946, 1952, National Council of the Churches of Christ, USA.
JBP – J. B. Phillips, *The New Testament in Modern English* © 1960 1972.

Typeset by Eagle Publishing.
Printed by:Cox & Wyman

ISBN 0 86347 075 0

For
David
With thanks to you and to God for
thirty-eight years of creative relating
and for
Mr and Mrs Huggy-bear
and
Mr and Mrs Tiggywinkle
with much love and the prayer
that we might all become
better conflict resolvers!

CONTENTS

RECOMMENDED READING

Cormack, Dr David, *Peacing Together* (MARC Europe, 1989).
*Cormack, Dr David, *Team Ministry* (MARC Europe).
Dennison, Justin, Team Ministry (London: Hodder & Stoughton, 1997).
(The above three books have excellent sections on both understanding conflict and its resolution.)

Augsburger, David, *Caring Enough to Hear and Be Heard* (Herald Press).
Augsburger, David, *Caring Enough to Confront* (London: Marshall Pickering).
Huggett, Joyce, *Listening to Others* (London: Hodder & Stoughton,1988).
Jacobs, Michael, *Swift to Hear* (London: SPCK,1985).
Long, Anne, *Listening* (London:DLT Daybreak, 1990).
(The books above help people improve their communication skills.)

*Mace, David and Vera, *Love and Anger in Marriage* (London: Marshall Pickering).
(Although this book was written with married couples in mind, its principles apply to all our relationships.) Other books on anger:
Augsburger, David, *Anger and Assertiveness in Pastoral Care* London: Fortress Press).
Campbell, Alistair V., *The Gospel of Anger* (London: SPCK).
A Symposium, *Be Angry and Sin Not* (Care and Counsel). A very useful introductory booklet on a complex subject.)
*Walters, Richard P., *Anger: What to Do About It* Leicester: (IVP).

Chave-Jones, Myra, *Listening to Your Feelings* (Oxford: Lion Publishing).
Moss, Edward, *Growing Into Freedom* (Guildford: Eagle).
(The above two books help us to understand and make sense of ourselves.)

Fowke, Ruth, *Personality and Prayer* (Guildford: Eagle).
Goldsmith, Malcolm and Wharton, Martin, *Knowing Me Knowing You* (London: SPCK).
Osborn, Lawrence and Diana, *God's Diverse People* (London: DLT Daybreak).
(The above three books open our eyes to the fascinating world of personality types and the implications on our life of the personality preferences we make. See also *Vision* magazine for details of Myers-Briggs courses that provide even more specific insights into this subject.)

Elmer, Duane, *Cross-Cultural Conflict* (Leicester: IVP).

For a series of daily Bible readings on the subject of conflict see:
Huggett, Joyce, *Learning the Language of Prayer* (Oxford: BRF).

* These books are now out of print. If you ever see them, they are well worth snapping up. They contain excellent material.

Acknowledgements

Writing a book is frequently likened to giving birth to a baby. It's a comparison that rings bells with me. So many people have supported me while I've been giving birth to this particular baby that I scarcely know who to thank first. Perhaps it should be my husband? David has been a tower of strength during this protracted labour. With endless patience he has read each version of each chapter. With sensitivity and skill, he has discussed the contents with me – pointing out the flaws as well as praising the parts he approves of. With care he has designed and drawn most of the diagrams that appear in the book. And he has done most of the cooking while I've been writing. To say that I am grateful is an understatement. To him I give the biggest bouquet.

David Wavre, Managing Director of Eagle, has also been hovering in the wings wondering when the baby would be born but cheering me on while he waited. To him, too, I want to say a huge thank you: for his trust, his kindness, his patience and his affirmation.

Members of the great Interserve family, the missionary organisation for which I work, have been more than conscious of the labour pains that have accompanied this birth. They have stood by and loved and prayed and I am humbled.

Many, many others, similarly, have prayed this book into being. I can't name you all. I don't even know you all but please be assured that I am profoundly thankful; grateful, too, for all those who have given me permission to share snippets of their story.

Finally I must thank the individuals who have

attended the Conflict seminars that David and I have led from time to time. Your affirmation, not to mention the love and laughter, have undoubtedly been the most enjoyable part of this particular pregnancy.

PREFACE

Two photographs stared out of the newspaper on the day I finished this book. One was of a volcano whose belly was belching out steam, ash and clouds of smoke; the other was of a British MP who was defiantly defending his decision to leave his wife and children to move in with his mistress. The two pictures, printed in close proximity with each other, seemed to summarise pictorially part of this book's message. For the book focuses on both the good news and the bad news about conflict. The bad news is that, just as molten lava and super-heated rock pouring from a volcano's mouth puts people in a panic and sets buildings ablaze, so unresolved conflict can and does destroy marriages and friendships, families and fellowships, businesses and churches and even missionary organisations.

A friend of mine once crystallised the situation with a pain-filled question. Reflecting on the ruptured relationship with his wife, he asked: 'How *can* two people who love each other end up hurting each other so badly?'

A missionary magazine similarly put the situation in a nutshell on one occasion by publishing a front cover that featured the startling imagethat appears at the top of the following page. The magazine's editorial claimed that one of the reasons why many missionaries return from the field sooner than they had originally intended is because they have never been provided with the tools that are needed to handle contaminated relationships. Consequently, they become so embittered and judgmental, discouraged and down-trodden that, eventually, they give up.

CONFLICT

> **One of the greatest impediments to reaching the unreached is failure to handle conflicts**

Because conflict batters and bruises beautiful people, because it frequently turns potentially powerful teams (whether secular or Christian) into veritable disaster areas, like countless others, I used to fear clashes and try to avoid them at all costs. There seemed to be something innately evil about the chaos conflict can create. Over the years, though, my views have undergone one radical re-think after another so that now I feel confident to spell out the good news – that conflict need not result in catastrophe. On the contrary, when individuals and groups take the trouble to understand its true nature and learn how to channel its energy creatively, slowly and over a prolonged period of time, like grit in an oyster, it can become a priceless pearl. This, at least, has become my personal experience over the twenty years since I first started to study the subject.

An invitation from Kingsway Publications in the early 1980s prompted me to martial my thoughts on the subject of conflict. The invitation was to write a book explaining why friction was tearing so many relationships to shreds and to suggest ways in which people might handle tension differently. The book, *Conflict, Friend or Foe?* was published in 1984. While it was still in its infancy, however, all copies were destroyed in a warehouse fire. Since that fire many would-be readers have asked why it has not been re-issued. The reason I consistently gave was: 'I want to revise it before it's re-printed.' I hadn't expected that the proposed revision would take years rather than weeks or maybe, at most, months but, with the wisdom of hindsight, I am glad that it did.

Since 1984 I have had the privilege of sitting along-side individuals and married couples, friends and groups while they have worked through conflict of one kind or another. By the grace of God, many of these individuals have been prepared so to work at the issues at stake that they have grown through the experience – and so have I. We continue to grow. Since the publication of the original book, too, I have had the privilege of sitting at the feet of others who have given more serious thought and more study time than I to the complex subject of conflict resolution. I am grateful to them for the richness of their seminar teaching, the challenge presented by their hand-outs and for enthusing me to read more extensively and widely. Since the publication of the original manuscript, then, I have devoured, with great appreciation and benefit, the books that are listed in the Recommended Reading List at the back of this book. The insights I have gleaned have challenged and enabled me to process inner conflicts of my own. They have also shown me, not simply how to cope when I clash with others but how to go on and on growing through the experience.

Growing Through Conflict, consequently is not the promised revision of *Conflict, Friend or Foe?* In that it uses a few of the illustrations from the original manuscript and processes them differently, this new book could, conceivably, be considered to be a sequel, though it does not assume that the reader has read the original book.

Growing Through Conflict begins, not with the bad news, but with the good news – that though conflict is an inevitable part of life, it has a positive face. In fact, the book begins by exposing ways in which Jesus himself grew through disagreements of various kinds. As chapter after chapter unfolds, we look together at some of the reasons why friction in relationships can be both full of pain and, at the same time, full of potential. We also observe ways of handling quarrels and collisions between people in a way that ensures they become the nerve-centre of growth.

Although the book underlines the friendly face of conflict and insists time and time again that conflict need not be an enemy but can rather become a faithful friend, I found writing it as much a harrowing as a healing experience. It was harrowing because it brought me face to face with areas of my own life that needed to be dealt with; yet it was healing because it provided me with fresh insight into ways of doing just that. It was harrowing because, to write a book of this nature with integrity demands that the author lives it; yet it was healing because working some of the insights into my own life and relationships is proving to be wonderfully cleansing and liberating. It was harrowing because of the spiritual warfare element involved yet it was healing because those closest to me sensed some of the struggle, cared – and prayed.

Just as writing the book was both harrowing and healing, so reading it could put the reader in touch with both despair and hope. For this reason, each chapter ends with some suggested exercises that I believe could rescue readers from simply gleaning a collection of insights on the subject of conflict's causes, complexities and resolution and provide them, in addition, with tools that, in the Creator's hands ensure that every clash contributes to the upbuilding rather than to the downfall of relationships. For this I pray, for I share

author Edward de Bono's beliefs that the costs of conflict can be so great that *any* improvement is worth
working for; that when we recognise the inadequacy of
our attitude to collisions in relationships, we can expect
considerable improvement and that 'there can be no
more important matter for the future of the world than
conflict resolution'.[1]

Joyce Huggett
Cyprus
16th September 1997

PART 1

Jesus:

Man of Conflict

1

THE FRIENDLY FACE OF CONFLICT

Conflict may be likened to the little girl in the nursery rhyme:

> There was a little girl
> Who had a little curl
> Right in the middle of her forehead
> When she was good
> She was very, very good
> But when she was bad
> She was horrid.

Conflict can be horrid: hurtful, harmful, disruptive of relationships and personal well-being. Dictionary definitions of the word hint at this. They remind us that the word 'conflict' is derived from two Latin words, *con* which means together and *fligere* which means to strike. The *Penguin English Dictionary* deduces from this that conflict means 'a struggle, a strong disagreement, a clash between contradictory impulses or wishes; to be incompatible, to oppose'. The *Chambers Dictionary* similarly claims that conflict means, 'a trial of strength between opposed parties or principles, a violent collision, a struggle or contest, a battle; to fight, contend, to be in opposition, to clash, to be at odds with . . .' A dictionary on the Internet insists that conflict means a 'state of disharmony between two incompatible persons, ideas or interests. A fight for supremacy.'

Such disharmony, such clashes, such violent collisions, such fights for supremacy, often over-power us with the suddenness and force of a tornado. They catch us off guard and leave such havoc in their wake that many Christians assume that conflict is innately sinful: something to confess.

But is this assumption correct? In *Team Ministry*, Justin Dennison challenges it by suggesting that conflict 'is neutral: (neither good nor bad); natural (not to be avoided or denied); normal (neither your particular problem nor necessarily your fault); and indeed healthy (part of being a human being)'. As such, conflict 'should be viewed as being common to all human relationships as people interact closely with each other'.[1]

He goes on to insist that our goal 'should not be to ensure the absence of conflict, but to be equipped with the ability to handle and resolve conflict in an honest and healthy way. It is *unresolved* conflict, not conflict as such, that can damage relationships.'[2]

Surely, Justin Dennison's observations must be correct? After all, Jesus was so frequently locked in conflict and, indeed, often initiated clashes that, for him, living with disharmony and disagreements could be said not only to be the norm but even necessary.

Conflict, then, cannot be innately sinful. Rather, it is the way we handle collisions and contests that determine whether or not sin creeps into the equation. Jesus' skilful handling of power struggles demonstrates the news that surprises some – that all conflict, whatever its source, is potentially creative. It is creative because it faces us with a choice: to respond in a way that strengthens and builds up relationships, promotes the Kingdom of God and causes the individuals concerned to grow in Christlikeness and maturity or to act and react in a way that disrupts friendships and fellowships, inner peace and integrity.

When we respond to conflict creatively, wisely and in a Christlike way, differences become like the little girl in the nursery rhyme: not simply good but very, very good.

The challenge that faces us in this book is to discover some answers to the million-dollar question, 'How on earth do we learn to respond to clashes and quarrels, disagreements and divisions in such a constructive, positive, creative way?'

One way is to watch the spotlight fall on Jesus so that he becomes our teacher in this, as in all things. That is why I devote the rest of this chapter and the next to a close scrutiny of Jesus, man of conflict.

Jesus: Man of conflict

'Jesus: man of conflict.' That title may strike some as strange. But is it? After all, did Jesus not claim: 'I did not come to bring peace, but a sword' (Matt 10:34)? Or, as Luke puts it: 'Do you think I came to bring peace on earth? No, I tell you [not peace], but division' (Luke 12:51). Or, as Eugene Peterson paraphrases Jesus' insistence:

'Do you think I came to smooth things over and make everything nice? Not so. I've come to disrupt and confront! From now on, when you find five in a house, it will be –

> Three against two, and two against three;
> Father against son,
>   and son against father;
> Mother against daughter,
>   and daughter against mother;
> Mother-in-law against bride,
>   and bride against mother-in-law.'

Jesus created conflict

From the moment of his conception, Jesus fleshed out this warning. Even the manner of his conception created division – initially between Joseph and Mary. Mary believed the message of the angel and marvelled at the mysterious, miraculous implantation in her womb of the Saviour-seed. Joseph, on the other hand, rejected Mary's claim that she was pregnant by the Holy Spirit. Understandably in the circumstances, he resolved to take the drastic action of setting in motion divorce proceedings. While Jesus was no more than a foetus, then, he was setting his earthly father against his mother. He was also stirring up within Joseph untold inner conflict as he wrestled with the question: 'Is Mary telling the truth or not?'

Jesus' birth triggered off yet more conflict: between the Magi and Herod, for example; between Herod and the parents in Bethlehem whose babies he butchered – and between the Jews and Jesus. In his Gospel, John likens the Jews-versus-Jesus contest to the incompatibility that exists between light and darkness. In his immortal prologue to the Gospel, he paints a picture of a world so engulfed by darkness that it has closed its heart to the light. When Light shone in the form of Jesus, therefore, the clash was inevitable and vicious. Although the world preferred its familiar dimness to the Light, its all-pervading, evil-polluted darkness could not extinguish *God's* glory: 'The Life-Light blazed out of the darkness; the darkness couldn't put it out' (John 1:4,5, *The Message*).

Little by little, the Light of Christ pushed back the darkness in rather the same way that dawn dispels the inky-dark night. Gradually, some people gravitated towards their Messiah and to all who received him, 'to those who believed in his name, he gave the right to become children of God ' (John 1:12–13).

In other words, for some of the Jews, as indeed for Joseph, their struggles had a friendly face in that they became like the fingers of God pointing at deeply ingrained attitudes and beliefs that needed to be changed.

Conflict worked similarly for Mary and for Jesus

himself. A clash of expectations and opinion with her twelve-year-old son showed Mary where she needed to change. It also contributed to her growth in understanding of her Son's God-given mission – that mission that is encapsulated in his name, Jesus; Saviour.

Twelve is a significant age for Jewish boys, both in Jesus' day and today. The onset of their teen years marks the beginning of a new phase of life when they are expected to take personal responsibility for their observance of the Law. At the same time, this new phase of life heralds a fresh awakening of personality, vocation and self-assertion.

Mary and Joseph take Jesus to Jerusalem to celebrate the Passover. There, the youthful Son of God whose unique, two-pronged mission is to reveal God's love and proclaim his reign senses an intensifying and quickening of his call. He moves into mission mode and consequently cannot bear to tear himself from the Temple – the place where the awareness of his Father's nearness and dearness is so acute and profound. His parents, though, far from being in mission mode with him, like all Middle Eastern villagers, are steeped in tradition. Their assumption is that, like the other children from Nazareth, Jesus has re-joined the caravan heading for home. After three days of hurry, worry and futile searching, they return to the Temple to find their charge alive with wonder, tingling with anticipation, full of excitement, lost in filial love – love for his *heavenly* Father. The result? A sharp altercation. Mary rebukes Jesus: 'Why have you done this to us? Your father and I have been half out of our minds looking for you' (Luke 2:48, *The Message*). Jesus retaliates with a cool, calm, collected question: '*Why* were you looking for me? Didn't you know I had to be here, dealing with the things of my Father? (Luke 2:49, emphasis mine).

Such clashes of expectation, opinion and vision, had they happened in some families, would have driven a wedge between parents and adolescents. Not so for the holy family. Although Mary and Joseph failed to understand Jesus' reasoning (Luke 2:50) and although they may even have been hurt because Jesus referred to *God* as Father whereas Mary applies the word 'father' to Joseph, it would appear that their relationship was deepened by the confrontation and not weakened. Mary returns home to ponder, to learn, to explore, to spread her confusion and her unknowing before God. Luke portrays her perfectly with one deft stroke of his pen: His mother treasured, that is, she 'held these things dearly, deep within her herself' (Luke 2:51, *The Message*). Not only has Mary mellowed, Jesus has changed too. He remains envisioned by his heavenly Father but, equally, is at pains to relate sensitively and obediently to his earthly parents and though he is now their young adult son rather than their child, to honour them. Conflict has caused both to change and to grow.

Were they aware as they settled back in their hillside home that there would be other occasions when Jesus and his family would clash openly? Whether they anticipated future battles or not, they happened. One obvious example is the wedding that Mary, Jesus and the disciples attended in Cana of Galilee. Middle Eastern weddings are large, joyous, long-drawn-out affairs where the wine flows freely. To run out of wine would be outrageous, discourteous, scandalous – the topic of scornful village gossip for months to come. Mary now seems wonderfully aware of her Son's mission and special gifting. At the same time, she continues to behave towards Jesus in the way most Middle Eastern mothers behave towards their unmarried sons: assuming the right to tell him what to do. She seems to insist that he performs a miracle – *now*. Jesus' public ministry has already begun. Again he confronts her with the clear implication: 'I must now be guided by God, not you.'

Was Mary crushed by this rebuke? Did the disciples overhear the conversation? Were they aware that, as men who now lived in community with Jesus, they would similarly be subjected to the fearless, constructive confrontation of this man in whose hands conflict became a teacher whose lessons were written on the heart in indelible writing?

'Who do people say I am?' he was soon to ask them (Mark 8:27). 'Who do *you* say I am?' he was to persist. Peter's answer was ready and spontaneous: 'You are the Christ' (Mark 8:29), but it soon became evident that, although Peter was partially enlightened, his new-found knowledge remained rooted in error. For him, 'the Christ' meant an earthly not a heavenly king. When Jesus began to spell out the truth – that he must suffer rejection and murder before his resurrection, Peter declared his true colours by rebuking him. Whereupon Jesus retaliated with a resounding: 'Peter, get out of my way! Satan, get lost! You have no idea how God works' (Mark 8:33, *The Message*).

Far from wasting this conflict, Jesus uses it to introduce a vital piece of teaching: that Jesus' disciples must share in his self-denial, rejection and cross, that they must face the challenge of building their lives, not on self-love but on God's love. In other words, Jesus used conflict in relationships as traffic controllers use red lights – to stop a relationship in its tracks – to prevent it from hurtling out of control, to rescue it from travelling in the wrong direction, to save it before it harmed others- and to re-negotiate it on a new set of terms.

Jesus battered by conflict

Jesus not only created conflict – within his family and within his community of hand-picked companions – throughout his public ministry he found himself embroiled in fierce cosmic conflict of the kind Paul describes: 'We are not fighting against human beings but against the wicked spiritual forces in the heavenly world, the rulers, authorities, and cosmic powers of this dark age' (Eph 6:12, GNB).

Indeed, Peter's rebuke seems to have triggered off in Jesus' mind the memory of that forty-day retreat he made in the Judaean Desert when he was pitchforked into vicious and bitter warfare with his arch-enemy, Satan.

Immediately after his baptism, at the very outset of his public ministry, while he's still saturated with the love and affirmation that has poured from his Father's heart into his own heart, God's Spirit thrusts him into the Judaean Desert – to have his strength and resolve tested. There, scorched and drained by the blistering, energy-sapping heat and further weakened by lack of food, Jesus is subjected to a most vicious attack of the evil one.

Jim Packer opens our eyes to the nature of this enemy when he writes: 'The Bible encourages us to believe in a Satan, and a host of Satanic myrmidons, who are of quite unimaginable badness – more cruel, more destructive, more disgusting, more filthy, more despicable, than anything our minds can conceive.'[3] This enemy's skill lies, partly, in knowing where and when to wound.

There in the desert, just as this malicious marauder had sidled alongside Eve centuries earlier, now the twister of the truth sidles alongside Jesus. Just as his ploys had resulted in such a resounding success when he pitted his wits against Eve, so he now schemes to knock God's Son off course.

Jesus has come with a clear mandate from his Father – to usher in a kingdom built on love that will eventually oust the kingdom mankind has built – on self. Jesus is a young man – just emerging from hiddenness to launch his God-entrusted ministry. 'How am I going to achieve my aims?' Was that a question that plagued him as he tuned into the political climate of the day? He quickly discerned the Jews' longing for a Messiah who would deliver them from the tyranny of their oppressors and who would restore Israel's former glory. Enter Satan. Just as, when he assaulted Eve, he used as his weapon a misrepresentation of God's own words to raise doubt in Eve's mind: 'Has God said . . .?' so now he comes to Jesus with the Father's words similarly moistening his lips. The Father has affirmed Jesus as his Son. Does Satan use the image of Sonship to inject into Jesus' mind and imagination and heart images that would appeal to the waiting throng and ensure him a swift and tumultuous following? Or is Satan here sowing seeds of doubt in Jesus' mind about his own status as Son? Is he, perhaps, pressing on some anxiety in Jesus that he might not gain credibility with the waiting crowd? Does he, in fact, whisper, '*If* you are God's Son . . . turn these stones into bread' or does he sneeringingly say a sarcastic, '*Since* you are God's Son . . . turn these flat, round, cream, pebble-like stones into pitta bread'? Whichever interpretation we place on the Gospel record, the temptation sounds so sensible, so plausible, so possible – especially if Jesus' mind moves into fast forward so that he pictures himself standing on the Galilean hillside multiplying two small loaves and five little fish in order to feed over five thousand people.

How long did he wrestle with Satan's seed-thoughts? How long did they allure him before he won the first round of the fight for supremacy? We are not told. We are told that, eventually, his mind, his heart, his imagination, his will, indeed his whole being recoiled at Satan's subtle suggestions. Being God's Son has nothing to do with using his God-entrusted power to gratify self, feather his own nest, seek self-glory, self-satisfaction or the praise of people. Being God's Son means trusting God's Word, feeding on it and living in intimate communion with the One he loves. It is about commitment, dedication and obedience. Far from being about self-aggrandisement or worldly pleasure, it is about pleasure of a different kind: the delight that comes through bringing joy to Another. It is about feasting on manna of a different kind – hence his rebuff: 'It takes more than bread to stay alive. It takes a steady stream of words from *God's* mouth' (Matt 4:4, *The Message*, emphasis mine).

Was Jesus exhausted by the time he had processed this inner conflict? Probably. As the writer to the Hebrews is at pains to tell us, he was tempted just as we are. Temptations rarely come gently, they seem to well up from the very core of our being in an all-consuming way, they beat against our wills in rather the same way as waves crash into rocks with all their frothing, foaming persistence. They create an inner turmoil that is not unlike the restless churning and raging of an angry sea. They persuade us that the only way calm will be restored is to cave in; to capitulate.

Although Jesus refused to capitulate, although round one of the contest clearly went to him, Satan refuses to give up. Rapidly, he moves in for the kill.

Just as he used the attraction she could see so vividly with her eyes to tempt Eve, now he tempts Jesus through the eyes of his imagination. He takes Jesus on an imaginary trip to the Temple in Jerusalem where he leads him to the platform that had been constructed on the Temple's pinnacle. Continuing to twist Jesus' title, 'Son of God', he goads God's Son a second time: 'If you are God's Son . . .'; 'Since you're God's Son, jump. After all, you're protected by angels. They'll catch you. You won't even "stub your toe on a stone" ' (Matt 4:6, *The Message*).

As we have already noted, Jesus is well aware of the expectations of the crowds that have flocked to John the Baptist for baptism. They eagerly await the one who will, they believe, be an extraordinary earthly king who will deliver them from the Romans and accomplish great feats. They would see him leap from the Temple's parapets. They would love it. The spectacle would confirm his unique Sonship. They would rally

28

round him, believe in him, support him. Again, the suggestion sounds so plausible, so sensible, so certain of ensuring success. Except for one thing. It clearly flew in the face of the God who had decreed: 'Don't you dare test the Lord your God' (Deut 6:16, quoted by Jesus in Matt 4:7, *The Message*).

We are not told how long Jesus wrestled with this temptation. Possibly for days on end, even weeks. Temptations like these rarely worm their way through one ear only to crawl straight out of the other. They lodge in our hearts and start a civil war raging in our wills. Their suggestions and counter-suggestions rant and rave back and forth, back and forth until we scarcely know what we really do want nor even what is right. Eventually, though, with the skill and strength of a man surfing on the crest of a gigantic wave, Jesus rallies. Silencing Satan with Scripture, he wins a second resounding victory over sin and the evil one himself. His determination neither to live for pleasure nor for popularity, neither for power nor for prestige but rather to devote his life to God – taking God at his word, doing God's work in God's way – has won him the victory.

Still Satan refuses to retreat. In the third round of the contest, the Prince of Peace is assailed by the 'prince of this world' – a title Jesus himself gave to his enemy. Was 'the chief of this godless world'[4] beguiled into believing that day that he was playing his irresistible trump card? After all, when he had played it in the game with Eve, he had won hands down. Since then, every man and woman who has walked this earth has displayed the longing that plunged Eve into ruin – the yearning 'to be as God' (Gen 3:6).

Joseph Neuner puts this persuasively:

'You will be like God.' This is what all people through the ages try to become by building their own kingdom in their own way. Most of them have to do it on a small scale within their little world, others succeed in extending it to ever wider dimensions. But the driving force and the root is the same: the human need for bread, the longing for glory and social status, the urge to dominate, the desire for power.[5]

Yes. The most grave and persuasive temptation that tugs at the heart of men and women of every race and every generation, the temptation that so easily ensnares us, is the determination to enthrone self – to ensure that self is the centre of the universe. Jesus came, however, with a clear mandate from the Father – to be different; to offer an alternative outlook and lifestyle: a life that revolves around God rather than around self. How does he feel, then, when the tempter has him dreaming of standing on the peak of a high mountain. Or does Satan literally lead him to the mountain peak? With an extravagant gesture, he ensures that Jesus' horizon is filled with the magnificent panorama that stretches before him – the breathtaking array of all the kingdoms of the world. 'They're yours – lock, stock and barrel. *Just go down on your knees and worship me, and they're yours'* (Matt 4:9, *The Message*, emphasis mine).

Satan seems to have overstepped the mark this time. 'Jesus' refusal was curt: "Beat it, Satan!" ' Quoting from Deuteronomy, he declares his own hand with its trump card: ' "Worship the Lord your God, and only him. Serve him with absolute single-heartedness" ' (v 10).

'The Test was over. The Devil left' (v 11). Was Jesus wrung out? Matthew seems to suggest that he was. Surely that is why, as Satan left, angels moved in – to take care of Jesus' needs. Any exhaustion seems to have been short-lived, however. Jesus had fought the fight to the bitter end. Not only had he won, he emerged from the experience empowered and equipped to serve. Conflict had forced him to make courageous choices, conflict had sharpened his motto, 'I will serve God with absolute single-heartedness', conflict had caused creative tension to throb through his veins: the kind of creative tension that pulsates through a woman in labour; the kind of persistent tension that refuses to give up until it has given birth to the new life about to burst forth. Strength, power, determination, the desire to do God's work in God's way burst forth from Jesus before he left the desert. At the end of his retreat, he strides forth – in the power of the Spirit (Luke 4:14), the same but strangely different. New. The newness of this power was conflict's gift to him – conflict's reward: conflict's friendly face.

Just as family conflict, community conflict and cosmic conflict shaped Jesus by chiselling away all that might mar the image of God he came to portray, so, if we will process it faithfully and skilfully, conflict with family and friends, friction in the fellowship and the neighbourhood and spiritual warfare will play its part in transforming us into the likeness of Christ.

Most of the conflict in which we find ourselves embroiled boils down to a contest between self-centredness and love: love of God and love of others. Whenever we find ourselves at loggerheads with another, then, it can be helpful to take time out to ask ourselves the kind of questions that appear in the following exercises.

Suggested exercises

1. How am I feeling about what is happening in this relationship at the moment? If we list the emotions, if necessary, choosing some from the list of 'feeling words' that appears at the end of this chapter, and then take a careful look at the words we have written or chosen, we can then process them by asking some further questions: 'What do these emotions show me about the desires of my heart? Am I want-

ing 'to be as God', to ensure that self is the centre of my universe, or am I really longing that my life should revolve around God and be dedicated to the service of others?'

2. What are these emotions reflecting back to me about the orientation of my life and my current life goals?

3. What are my reactions to current conflict telling me about the values that drive me at this moment in time?

3. How have past conflicts been like the little girl in the nursery rhyme – not just good but very, very good because they have shown me how to become more like Jesus?

Some 'Feeling' Words

abandoned
accepted
affectionate
afraid
anxious
appreciated
bewildered
battered
cheated
concerned
contented
confused
defeated
depressed
dejected
delighted
disappointed
dejected
delighted
disappointed
dominated
embarrassed
envious
excited
exhilarated
fearful
feminine
frigid
frustrated
grateful
gratified
guilty
glad
happy

helpless
hopeless
hostile
hurt
hypocritical
ignored
inadequate
incompetent
icy
inferior
inhibited
involved
isolated
invigorated
jealous
judgemental
joyful
jolly
lonely
lovable
loving
loyal
manipulated
masculine
misunderstood
moody
marvellous
merry
needy
nasty
old
optimistic
overlooked
passionate

peaceful
pessimistic
phoney
pleased
possessive
pressurised
proud
rejected
repelled
rewarded
sad
secure
shallow
silly
stupid
suspicious
sympathetic
tender
terrified
threatened
two-faced
ugly
unappreciated
unresponsive
uptight
used
useless
victimised
vengeful
violent
weary
weepy
youthful

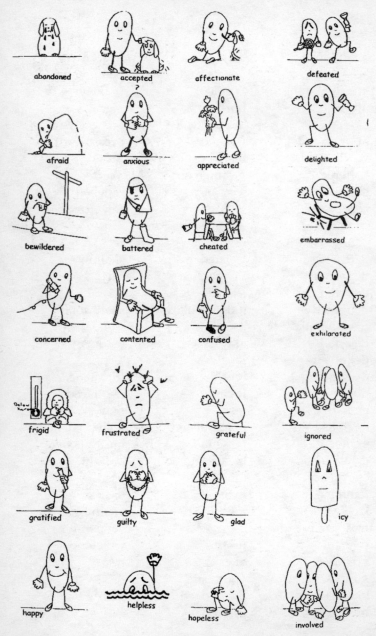

abandoned   accepted   affectionate   defeated

afraid   anxious   appreciated   delighted

bewildered   battered   cheated   embarrassed

concerned   contented   confused   exhilarated

frigid   frustrated   grateful   ignored

gratified   guilty   glad   icy

happy   helpless   hopeless   involved

Drawings by Pat Bish

2

INNER CONFLICT

Conflict, of itself, is not sinful. Conflict, of itself, is natural, normal, neutral, often necessary. Because it can become the finger of God that beckons us to re-evaluate our attitudes and re-examine our goals and because it can be to our relationships what an amber light is to traffic – the reminder that we need to slow down, to pause at life's crossings – it can contribute to our growth in Christlikeness. We reached these conclusions in chapter one by turning the spotlight on Jesus, the man of conflict. In this chapter, we continue to tease out the implications of handling conflict the Jesus-way.

Since life, for Jesus, seems to have been a constant round of battles of one kind or another, he has much to teach us. Our need to learn is urgent. After all, Jesus warned that following him would catapult *us* onto a collision course: evangelists with the evangelised (Matt 10:14), hosts with guests (v 14), brothers with each other (v 21), children with parents (v 21), God-fearers with God-haters (v 23), and so on.

Jesus clearly grew through such clashes as we noted in chapter one – through the titanic struggle with Satan, through disagreements with his mother, through being at odds with the disciples, through opposing the religious leaders of his day. If we are to emulate him, however, we must dig deep below the surface and recognise that his life was not merely a round of inter-personal struggles (conflict with other people) nor a round of inter-group contests (clashes between the Scribes and the Pharisees or the Pharisees and his disciples) nor even a round of spiritual battles as he continued to wage war with his arch-enemy, Satan. The most persistent and pernicious conflict for Jesus, as for Eve before him, was not the battering that came from outside of himself but the inner turmoil that frequently disturbed his equilibrium. Reflecting on the turmoil that tore Eve to shreds, David Cormack observes:

> In the garden of Eden, Eve was made aware of a choice, one which involved irreconcilable tensions – to believe what her God had said, or to yield to her own desires to be different. The conflict was not between her and the Tempter; rather it was between what she was and what she might become. It was an inner conflict. *Most conflict is inner conflict.* It causes more stress and more hurt than all the physical forms of conflict put together . . .[1]

Inner conflict clearly caused Jesus untold hurt and stress. Whereas, as we observed in chapter one, he seemed to ride, exhilarated, on the crest of a gigantic wave in the final round of his wilderness contest against Satan, when faced with the challenge of combating his own emotions, such waves could knock him off-balance and threaten to drown him.

Jesus acknowledged and owned his feelings

I am thinking, for example, of his own admission in the garden of Gethsemane on that crisp, cold, cruel night before his crucifixion. Taking his three most trusted companions deep into the seclusion of the gardens he loves, he begs them to stay with him; to watch, to pray because: 'the sorrow in my heart is so great that it almost crushes me' (Matt 26:38, GNB).

In the weeks and days and hours that have led up to

this moment, Jesus has been pounded, not by one wave of sorrow and rejection but by the surge and swell of one gigantic wave after another. The result is that he has now been dashed to the ground and pinned there. With disarming honesty and endearing transparency, he refuses to hide his conflicting emotions. Instead, he exposes them – in true Middle Eastern style. Men in the Middle East do not comply with the stiff-upper-lip mentality of men in the West. If they are sad, they weep openly and unashamedly; if they feel anxious, they divulge the reason why they are troubled; if they are happy, they show it by walking with a spring in their step or by the broad smile that creases their face. Jesus was a Middle Easterner.

John, Jesus' closest friend, picks up the innuendoes well when he recalls the events that took place in the Upper Room prior to Jesus' collapse in the garden of Gethsemane.

Jesus comes to the Upper Room traumatised, on the one hand, by the awful ache created by the impending farewell that he must say to his much-loved disciples and overjoyed, on the other hand, by the anticipation that soon, very soon, he is to be united with his Father (John 13:1 and John 14:28). In other words, he comes with a divided heart; with conflicting loyalties. He comes, too, feeling to the full, on the one hand, the terrible sting of rejection: the rejection of Peter who opposes the gesture of love he makes by protesting when Jesus attempts to wash his feet; the rejection of Judas whose cool, calculated, step-by-step, irreversible treachery is patently clear to Jesus; the forthcoming denial of Peter whose bravado this night has such a hollow ring about it; the forthcoming fear that will consume the rest of his friends and add wings to their feet as they flee from him instead of staying alongside him when he most needed them; feeling to the full, on the other hand, the deep, inextinguishable loyalty and love that will always bind him to these men with whom he has shared so much.

When we lurch from the grief of impending good-byes to the elixir of anticipated reunion, from the scourge of felt rejection to an in-touchness with committed love, albeit love bruised, we consume a great deal of energy. And there is more, so much more emotion flooding Jesus' entire being that night. This man whose heart is already torn in two assumes the guise of a slave and displays 'the full extent of his love' (John 13:1) which he pours into his disciples' hearts as he plunges their sweaty, dust-covered feet in refreshing water. Most costly of all, in the middle of supper, he rises from the table and continues to express the plenitude of his felt love by giving them two more priceless, parting gifts. First, he holds high the Passover loaf. Next he raises the goblet of blood-red wine. With those immortal, awesome words that neither they nor we can fully comprehend, he offers these gifts to them, begging them to receive them so that he might be in them and they in him:

'This is my body . . .
This is my blood . . .
Take, eat . . . drink'

What does it cost him to anticipate by this symbolism the supreme sacrifice that he is about to make? No one can answer that question. We can only surmise that, emotionally, it cost him not less than everything.

Emptied of all but love, wrung out, he reaches the garden of Gethsemane where we discover the secret of his strength. Here he hides nothing. Instead, he pours into his Father's listening ear the full gamut of his emotions: his desires, his dreads, his fears. Here a series of tidal waves, bigger and more terrifying than those we mentioned earlier, beat upon his body and his soul with all their terrifying might. His heart and mind and will struggle between two options: should he, could he, say yes to the Father's plan that he should now hand over the controls of his life to his enemies and allow himself to be led to that place where he would rather not go: Golgotha; or should he, could he flesh out that resolve with which he came into the world, 'I have come to do your will, O God' (Heb 10:7)? Just as that motto was reinforced in the Temple when he, the twelve-year-old was locked in conflict with his mother and just as it was brought into sharp focus in the Judaean Desert at the beginning of his public ministry when he clashed with Satan, so now it is intensified by the inner conflict that tosses him this way and that. As Jesus pours out his pain, peace descends and prevails. The circumstances do not change but Jesus' heart is changed. He says the 'yes' that enables him to achieve more in the next three days than he has accomplished in the three years since his public ministry began. He utters that 'yes' that fills him with the transparent power and majesty and authority that overpowers his oppressors when they arrest him in the garden. So, when Judas leads the armed, lantern-carrying detachment of soldiers and the cluster of chief priests and Pharisees to Jesus, knowing that they had come to arrest him, Jesus rises to greet them:

'Who is it you want?' he asks.

'Jesus of Nazareth,' they reply

'I am he,' answers Jesus.

When Jesus utters the words, ' "I am he," they *drew back and fell to the ground*' (John 18:6, emphasis mine).

Jesus takes his inner conflict to his Father

What is the secret of Jesus' strength and poise, majesty and recovery? What has brought about this dramatic growth in him? Aware of the inner turbulence that is tossing him first one way and then another, he identifies and names before the Father the opposite and opposing emotions that are threatening to sever his very soul. Having named and owned his terror, his dread and his ingrained resistance to the Father's will, he pauses. He reflects. He agonises. His resources replenished, he rallies. With integrity, he can now reiterate that motto that has governed his whole life, 'Not my will but yours be done.' Once again, he is highly motivated to complete his mission – the redemption of the world.

How long did it take him to recover? We are not told. What was the secret of his recovery? As I ponder the mystery of the latter question, I turn, from time to time, to 'The Dynamic Cycle of Being and Well-Being' that British psychiatrist, Frank Lake, developed.

Dynamic Cycle of Being and Well-Being[2]

The model illustrates the need we all have for acceptance by someone who will come to us personally when we are becalmed by need. The model shows, too, how dependent we are on this source and resource person for sustenance at every level of our being: social, spiritual, emotional, mental . . . When we know we are uniquely accepted, we become increasingly secure in 'just being'; confident that we are special, not for anything we achieve but simply because we are. And when every part of our being is nourished, a sense of well-being percolates around us re-energising and re-motivating us. Little by little we learn who we are. The 'knowing' gives us such a sense of well-being that, in turn, energy surges from the well-springs of our heart into every part of our being and overflows from us to others: other people and other projects.

What appears to be happening in Gethsemane is that Jesus comes to his Father full of fear and dread, as we have seen. He empties his emotions into the lap of the God who accepts him *with* the fear, *with* the dread, *with* the reluctance to obey. With God's ready acceptance comes the sustenance Jesus craves. Emotionally and spiritually, Jesus knows himself resourced by God. His sense of well-being is renewed. Reassured of his status as God's Son, he finds himself revitalised – ready to rise to the challenge of paying the price of achieving the salvation of the world.

Jesus knew what to do in the extremity of his need that night before he died because, throughout his public ministry, he had established a pattern of making frequent recourse to the Father. There, he seems to have received so much acceptance, affirmation and sustenance that he regularly emerged from the Father's presence highly motivated, indeed, brimful of dynamic energy which, in turn, achieved so much for others.

Towards the beginning of his Galilean ministry, for example, we watch him facing the challenge of holding in tension the joy his disciples were expressing at the 'success' of their first mission and the anguish that must have filled his heart as he processed the news of his cousin's brutal murder. His response is to seek solitude.

What does he do in the deafening silence of the mountainside late that afternoon? Almost certainly he expresses his inner turmoil, including his grief, to his Father. Almost certainly he finds himself sustained by the Father's love. Certainly, he lingers in his Father's loving presence. Consequently, that evening, we observe him re-energised. Bursting with divine energy, he strides across the Sea of Galilee lovingly to rescue his frazzled, frightened disciples. As he was to explain to the disciples months later, 'I've loved you the way my Father has loved me' (John 15:9, *The Message*).

As then, so now in the garden of Gethsemane. By taking his conflicting emotions to his Father, he processes them and grows in stature and obedience as a result. In other words, for Jesus, inner conflict always seems to have been homework to be done in the company of his Father rather than pressure to be ignored. He is, indeed, our teacher.

Taking *our* inner conflict to God

'In the world you will have trouble,' Jesus warned us (John 16:33). In other words, just as he was pounded by wave after wave of rejection, disappointment, frustration, pain, so we will frequently find ourselves lashed by waves that threaten to drown us. As we noted earlier in this chapter, the most overpowering waves are the waves of our own emotions. Someone hurts us. Anger sweeps through our entire being with terrifying force. Unable to control it, we hit out at anyone nearby. Or disappointment, even betrayal, batters us, knocking our heart to the ground. We look for support in this direction and that and find none. Inwardly crushed, we weep bitter, inner tears of helplessness and hopelessness.

At such times, we do well to emulate the pattern of Jesus: to recognise, name, own and reflect on our emotions, to spread them before the God who comes to us as silently but surely as the sun slides over the mountain range at sunrise, to dwell in his presence until an awareness of his understanding, accepting love trickles into the hurt or touches the panic, soothes the rejection or speaks into the dismay, the discomfort, the despair. Peter encourages us to do just this, 'Cast all your anxiety on him,' he invites. Be assured, with a deep-down assurance that 'he cares for you' (1 Pet 5:7).

Whenever we do this, we may not simply experience his acceptance as he whispers words like, 'You are precious in my eyes and I love you' (Is 43:4), just as he sustained Jesus, we may experience him feeding us. Just as he sent an angel to minister to Jesus in the wilderness and again in the garden of Gethsemane, so he will send others to minister to us – with a word of encouragement, maybe, or with a thank you. Sometimes his own whisper or felt love, experienced by a spiritual form of osmosis or intravenous feeding, will be enough to assure us that we are cherished. The initiative is his. The process demands little effort from us – just the willingness to relax in his presence.

When *we*, like Jesus, have experienced the in-flow of the Father's acceptance and sustenance, we, too, will find ourselves motivated to reach out to others. When others are hurting, we will long to go to them with the same kind of love that we, ourselves, have received. Our longing to serve God in whatever way he wants is renewed. Paul paints the picture powerfully: 'All praise to the God and Father of our Master, Jesus the Messiah! . . . He comes alongside us when we go through hard times, and before you know it, he brings us alongside someone else who is going through hard times so that we can be there for that person just as God was there for us' (2 Cor 1:3, *The Message*).

What a far cry this is from the way most of us handle inner conflict. Unlike Jesus, most of us neglect to take time out to process our emotions and to bring them to God. Instead, recognising our craving for acceptance, most of us fall into the trap of expecting others to provide it. We consequently place unbearable pressure on friends or spouse, fellowship group or pastor, teacher or mentor, counsellor or colleague. As Henri Nouwen explains, however, this is a recipe for disaster: 'No friend or lover, no husband or wife, no community or commune will be able to put to rest our deepest craving for unity and wholeness. And by burdening others with these divine expectations, of which we ourselves are often only partially aware, we evoke instead feelings of inadequacy and weakness.'[3]

Disillusioned by the inability of those closest to us to meet the deepest longings of our hearts or to cure our existential loneliness, we travel round Frank Lake's Dynamic Cycle of Being and Well-Being in the opposite direction from Jesus.

Egged on by our need for acceptance, we exhaust ourselves by seeking to buy it with our achievements. Unlike Jesus, who flatly refused to over-achieve and did and said only those things his Father told him to do and say (John 5:19, 30, 36; 8:29; 10:36–37), we *do* attempt to achieve too much.

Because we attempt to over-achieve, we fall into a variety of traps. The first is that of believing that our many and impressive accomplishments bestow on us a certain status. The second is failing to acknowledge that this status is self-generated, not given. The third is the trap of seeking self-generated sustenance and consequently of presenting ourselves to the world as those who are worthy of acceptance. To our dismay, though, the much-sought-after acceptance may not be forthcoming. The Dynamic Cycle of Being and Well-Being then becomes a treadmill. Endlessly, we travel round and round the circle in the opposite direction from Jesus, burning out badly in the process.

Another trap is that of pushing our emotions into the Pandora's box of the soul ensuring, of course, that the lid of the box is kept strictly and firmly locked. While ramming home our emotions in this way, we continue to trudge round the circle failing to recognise that the dynamic cycle has become, for us, a vicious circle that will need to be broken at some stage if we are to thrive rather than merely to survive.

The Vicious Circle

Is this why Justin Dennison makes this extraordinary claim:

> Inner conflicts . . . do not just affect ourselves, our own peace of mind, but inevitably, they spill over into our relationships with others, particularly when we draw close to others, as in marriage or in team ministry.
>
> If there is conflict between people, the first area to explore is not the *inter*-personal situation alone. Begin by exploring the possibility of *intra*-personal struggles [that is, personal struggles, inner conflict, opposing and contradictory inner voices that clamour for attention]. More often than not, the two are linked.[4]

How inner conflict affects relationships

They are linked for a number of reasons. Every person who walks this earth experiences within themselves stark contrasts: good and evil, light and darkness, love and hatred, strengths and weaknesses. Paul puts this powerfully:

> I know that all God's commands are spiritual, but I'm not. Isn't this also your experience? . . . What I don't understand about myself is that I decide one way, but then I act another, doing things I absolutely despise . . . I know the law but still can't keep it . . . the power of sin within me keeps sabotaging my best intentions . . . I decide to do good, but I don't *really* do it; I decide not to do bad, but then I do it anyway. My decisions, such as they are, don't result in actions. Something has gone wrong deep within me and gets the better of me every time.
> It happens so regularly that it's predictable. The moment I decide to do good, sin is there to trip me up. I truly delight in God's commands, but it's pretty obvious that not all of me joins in that delight. Parts of me covertly rebel, and just when I least expect it, they take charge.
> I've tried everything and nothing helps. I'm at the end of my rope.
>
> (Rom 7:21 ff, *The Message*)

Is there a single Christian who cannot identify with Paul's lament? We are all 'divided people'; 'people in conflict'.[5] As Myra Chave-Jones explains the situation:

> Many of us will be very aware of having some inner weakness that constantly lets us down. We may pray about it frequently. We may sometimes weep in despair. It may be to do with drink, sexual habits, money, a jealous attitude, a constant fear of rejec-

tion, a sense of inadequacy or inferiority, or anything that makes its presence felt in a disturbing
way. Sometimes there is a 'victory' at a great cost,
and the next time a dispiriting defeat. The weakness
cannot be corrected by a simple act of the conscious
will. It is an example of a problem in our 'psyche'
. . . [It is] the 'smoke' that signals a fire in the inner
life.[6]

We are not only divided people who sometimes live
life God's way and who are frequently tripped up by
the primitive, raw instincts that drive our thought life
and secret behaviour, we are also hurting people –
those who have been sinned against as well as those
who have sinned. We have all been buffeted by life in
one way or another. We carry round in our hearts the
legacy of the inner hurts we have sustained in the
recent or the far distant past. Many of these hurts (particularly those inflicted on us in childhood), remain
hidden but unhealed; hidden but not inactive. They
cause us to react to life from a hurting rather than from
a healed heart.

Take Marian and Joy, for example: firm friends.
Marian was married; Joy was single. They both led
busy, fulfilled lives but had many things in common:
walking, a love of nature, a longing for solitude, an
enjoyment of music. Joy appreciated spending an
evening in Marian's home as much as Marian valued
visiting Joy.

Whenever they were together their minds and
hearts seemed to meet. After years of bringing up children when the long days were filled with 'baby-talk', it
felt so good to Marian to spend quality time with someone like Joy who was steeped in the world of ideas.

Marian could never put her finger on one reason
why the relationship began to deteriorate. 'As far as I
can recall, it all goes back to one phone call,' she told
me. 'Joy seemed so different. So cold. I'd upset her for

some reason and the way she spoke to me just creased me. When I put the phone down, I burst into tears. After that, I wept for days and days. Then my husband got angry. "The friendship's not worth it," he said. "Forget it." But the friendship really matters to me. I don't want to forget it. And anyway, I want to find out the reason for this childish behaviour of mine. Right at this moment, Joy has withdrawn from me and I find myself hating her for that. But I know that, as a Christian, I shouldn't store up bitterness. I want to be rid of all these negative feelings.'

'Marian, does Joy remind you of anyone in your past? Mother maybe? Or father? Are her looks, mannerisms, tone of voice, reminiscent of an authority figure?'

Marian paused before saying, 'It's funny you should ask that. I've sometimes thought, after Joy's gone, that it's been just like talking to my mother – just the way it was when I was a little girl.'

Marian then surprised herself by pouring out the intense, deep-seated hatred for her mother that she had carried around with her, unacknowledged, since she was a child – the same sort of unmanageable bitterness she now felt towards Joy. One simple question had exposed the root of her rotting relationship with Joy.

Such tangles are not rare. They are common. We seek to relate closely with a particular person. Although we do not realise it, that person or situation produces a flash-back, albeit subconsciously, to a relationship with someone in the past – someone we feared, perhaps, someone we resented or someone to whom we felt hostile. At the time when these feelings first created havoc, maybe as far back as childhood, maybe in adolescence, maybe in early or more recent adulthood, we stuffed them into the store-house of our heart. There, they hid, like a virus in a computer. They hid but they did not die. When a relationship in the present is somehow so reminiscent of the original relationship that it produces an echo in our heart, the feelings corrupt our thinking and paralyse our behaviour in rather the same way as a virus corrupts computer files or causes the computer to crash. Their stored-up, destructive, terrifying energy is suddenly unleashed.

In Marian's case it was the hidden hatred and stored-up bitterness she felt towards her mother that was being re-activated as her relationship with Joy disintegrated. She was also bringing to the friendship the insecurity, lack of self-worth and fear of contradicting that the dysfunctional–relationship had engendered. At times, Marian was not relating to Joy at all, but to her mother. So there were times when she felt incapable of acting as an adult and resorted, instead, to the childish behaviour patterns to which she seemed to be chained. Although she despised herself for doing so, she found herself reacting to Joy in precisely the same way as she used to react to her mother – the one with whom to disagree was to risk forfeiting so-called 'love'.

Other people react to these transference experiences, as psychologists describe this linking of the present with the past, in a totally different way. Instead of repeating the reactions of the past, they reverse them. So the member of a music group who, from force of circumstances, was refused permission to challenge his authoritarian father even in his teenage years, may hit out, at least verbally, at the leader of the group if his leadership-style seems authoritarian. Or, as we are witnessing in today's society, young people whose relationships with parents or teachers have been full of criticism, nagging and put-downs may well hit out later in life at any and every authority figure: the police, the government, their immediate superior at college or at work and, of course, their 'boss'.

Others of us react to people and relationships and situations from the cess-pit of our own, often unrecognised or unacknowledged, loneliness. We, too, suffer from such a sense of insecurity or lack of self-esteem that it spills over, one way or another, into every relationship we attempt to make. Instead of being able to reach out to others in love, as Jesus did, because we dislike ourselves, even believe ourselves to be unlovable, we doubt that others will ever want to offer us love, so we withdraw from others rather than run the risk of being rejected by them. Instead of meeting other's needs, then, our own needs pre-occupy us compelling us to withdraw into our shell. Afraid that others will dislike us, we refuse to reveal our true feelings. Because we fear even a hint of criticism and are equally incapable of receiving praise and encourage-ment, we may become as prickly as hedgehogs, as quiet as mice or as aggressive as boxers – people who compete in the arena of life; people who strive to prove that they are as good, if not better than the next person.

Although we wear masks to camouflage all this inner activity, the energy we attempt to hide refuses to keep quiet. So, if a friend, a member of the family, someone in the fellowship or someone else lets us down, forgetting to post a letter, perhaps, or failing to keep an appointment, the emotional outburst with which we respond shocks us by its intensity as much as it astonishes others.

Or a married couple, who keep clashing can work so hard at concealing their distress that they become attention seekers by making excessive demands on others. Alternatively, they can exhaust themselves by over-much socialising because, they insist, we must 'have fun'. Or their need to be needed becomes so all-consuming that they manipulate people and situations to ensure that leadership roles are given to them whether or not they possess the necessary gifts to exercise that leadership effectively and well. As Myra Chave-Jones shrewdly observes: 'It is so much easier to wear the mask of competence than to be seen to be needy.'[7]

It *is* easier, certainly. But such campaigns do not

result in healing. They lead us deeper and deeper into neurosis and persuade us to wear masks that camouflage our true self and that, in turn, project a phoney self whose image we then have to strive to keep up.

How can we prevent our inner conflicts from spilling over into relationships and governing our lives in such inappropriate ways? One way is to take a step back from troublesome relationships, pause before God, ask for a fresh touch from the Holy Spirit, the one whose role it is to lead us into all truth (John 16:12) and ask the following questions:

- Have I ever encountered a situation like this before?
- Is there anything about this person or the relationship that reminds me of the past or of a previous relationship? (Mannerisms, tone of voice, attitude to life, facial expression, eyes, gestures, method of conducting friendships, name, role.)
- Am I relating only to the person present or have the edges become blurred so that I am, at the same time, relating to 'ghosts' of the past?
- Are my reactions and the force of them consistent with what is going on in this friendship or are they exaggerated? What might this be telling me?

Another way of preventing inner conflicts from contaminating our relationships and from governing our lives is to recognise, as Jesus did, that inner conflicts are homework to be done, not nuisances to muzzle and banish. Yet another way is to emulate him by coming to God in the quiet and begging for his help in processing our feelings.

Suggested exercises
Before reading on, you might like to try processing your feelings in one or more of the following ways:

1. Find a quiet place where you can relax. In your

imagination, watch an action replay of the past twenty-four hours. As you do so, tune into the various mood-swings and attitudes that punctuated your day. List them in contrasting pairs:

> *gratitude* and *meanness*
> *childlike delight* and *irritation*
> *hope* and *hurting*

Enjoy the positive, creative memories. Relive and relish them. Hand the uncomfortable attitudes and feelings to God, then become as still in your spirit as you can. Be aware of the coming of God. Open yourself to him. Let him breathe his Spirit into you afresh. Let him love you anew. Hear him whisper, not words of condemnation, but of love. See him holding the actions and reactions you regret as though they are as precious as cut crystal. Let him show you what gave birth to the meanness, the irritation or the pain. Maybe it was fear? Maybe it was concern for a loved one? Maybe it was perceived or actual rejection? Maybe it was the need to set certain boundaries so that you safeguard time for him?

As we have observed already in this chapter, Jesus has experienced all of these feelings. Let him come to you. Listen to what he says. Watch what he does. Respond to him as you will. Take your time. In his presence, there is no need to rush. Discover for yourself how wonderfully healing it can be simply to linger in his presence; to bask in his love.

Or open your mind afresh to the objective truth. In Christ, we are accepted. Jesus calls us his friends (John 15:15). In him we live and move and have our being (Acts 17:28). Because of Jesus, God whispers to us what he said to the Israelites of old: 'You are precious and honoured in my sight and . . . I love you' (Is 43:4).

Think of the Dynamic Cycle of Being and Well-

Being. Marvel and glory in the fact that God accepts you as you are. Marvel, too, at the nature of the divine sustenance. Jesus feeds us with himself: the Bread of Life. He invites us to come to him, to feast on his written Word, to receive the symbols of his body and blood in the bread and wine at Holy Communion. He fills us with his Spirit – and with all joy and hope in believing. Open your hands to receive his unique manna.

As you open your mind and your hands, what is your heart response? Do you thrill afresh at the real-isation that your status as a child of God has been secured? If so, thank God. If not, tell God what your feelings really are. If a sense of well-being fills you, you may find yourself wanting to serve God afresh. If so, ask him what it is that he wants you to do with your life – then do it.[8]

At first, to come to God in this way may seem strange, even foreign. Over a period of time, though, for many of us, it becomes the most natural thing in the world: a vital part of our day.

2. Sometimes, however, the inner conflict that tears us apart is so acute or we are so tired or distraught that we cannot find *words* to tell God what is on our hearts. At such times, I find it helpful to take some paper and a packet of felt-tip pens or pastels or paint sticks to my quiet place and to let different colours symbolise different emotions. Perhaps purple will represent pain, for example while pink may depict tenderness. There is no need to be particularly artis-tic to benefit from expressing feelings in this way. Our aim is not to produce a replica of a Rembrandt but rather to spread at God's feet the mixture of emotions that delight and distress us and to pave the way for him to come to minister to us *in* the con-flict.

3. Most introverts lap up opportunities like this to own and reflect on their feelings. For them, the whole process is therapeutic. Extraverts, on the other hand, may well prefer, and, indeed *need* to find a trusted friend with whom to share their feelings. If the friend is a Christian, after the two have talked, there is value in being still before God together, mentioning to him those things that have been shared.

4. There are as many other ways of naming, owning and reflecting on our feelings as there are people. Graham Millar suggests the following three:
'Write your own response to the following:
• Today, I struggle with feelings of _____.and _____
• I get really mad about _____
• Picture a hurt, a grief, a regret that is important in your life now. Hold it in focus, feel its effects. Now, picture God, as Jesus, coming into that scene. Watch what happens.[9]

Alternatively, David Cormack invites us to respond to questions like the following:
• How much conflict is in my world at the moment?
• Is my private world in disarray?
• Am I under pressure from surrounding and inner conflicts?
• How do I intend to restore my inner peace so that I can be of help to others?[10]

In *Tracks in the Sand*, Vance and Bethyl Shepperson give yet more options:
• 'Read Hebrews 11:1–12:14. When you have finished reading, close your Bible and close your eyes. Imagine yourself seated among this great cloud of witnesses, this circle of spiritual encouragers. You are surrounded by people from all the ages, the angels, and God. You know they are all watching

you from a heavenly grandstand as your life unfolds on Earth. Each failure from you brings a sympathetic groan from each of them. Each act of restraint or faith brings a roar of praise. These many witnesses of your life, as well as your Heavenly Parent, want you to take them inside yourself. They want to become your inner support system and function as loving, caring parents different from the ones you were given at birth. They promise love, nourishment, and healthy discipline that will enable you to heal, grow, and flourish.

Slowly open your eyes and open your journal. Write what it felt like to be in this circle of heavenly supporters. Include what you saw, heard, and felt. Give words to what you wanted to say to these people, to the angels, and to God. If you found it difficult to join the heavenly support group, write about how hard it was for you. When you have recorded your experience fully, close your journal and take a fifteen minute break before continuing the exercise.

Open your journal again and write a letter to yourself from one of your heavenly supporters. Choose one person with whom you most identify from the list of heroes and heroines in Hebrews 11. Pretend you are the hero or heroine you have selected. Write a letter to your failed self again, only this time it is from the vantage point of this biblical person. If you cannot identify with any of the people from the Hebrews' passage, choose someone from your own past who was an important source of encouragement and nurture. The letter your encourager is about to write must communicate support and firmness.

For example, such a letter might read:
"I'm Moses. Even though I was a murderer, God used me to liberate my people from slavery. I know what it is like to be a slave and so do you. You never need go back into slavery again because I know you

God. Don't give in to _____ God has better plans for you than that . . . I, Moses, a former slave, will be here for you to remind you of the power of God to liberate you."

• When you have finished this letter, write a letter back to your heavenly supporter. Let this letter come from your heart, from the failed self who is always afraid of blowing it . . . After you have finished your return letter, close your eyes and imagine hearing words of encouragement from your heavenly supporter. Let your self feel comforted and soothed. Hear the words of gentle, firm discipline that communicate genuine love and caring.

• Open your eyes and jot in your journal the words of encouragement you heard.'[11]

When we discover creative ways like these that enable us to process the jumble of emotions that drive us, although inner conflict may continue to *feel* horrid, in the language of the nursery rhyme I quoted at the beginning of this book, it will, in fact contribute to our growth and in that sense become a gift – something very, very good.

PART 2

Understanding

Conflict

3

THE TAPROOT OF UNRESOLVED CONFLICT

Conflict between Christians is to be expected. Jesus warned us that it would erupt for us as it did for him. Conflict can feel horrid while, at the same time, so working on behalf of our growth that it becomes like the little girl in the nursery rhyme – very, very good. That's what we observed in the last two chapters. Even so, many of us find ourselves shocked to discover Jesus' disciples 'bickering over who of them would end up the greatest' (Luke 22:24, *The Message*), stunned, too, to accept the fact that one of the biggest problems facing fellowships at home and missionaries working overseas today is the conflict that threatens to divide Christian from fellow Christian.

But is this so surprising? Think of that salutary little sentence in Acts where Luke puts this on record: Paul and Barnabas (the first missionaries) 'had such a sharp disagreement that they parted company' (Acts 15:39).

The cause of the problem? 'Paul said to Barnabas, "Let's go back and visit all our friends in each of the towns where we preached the Word of God . . ." Barnabas wanted to take John . . . nicknamed Mark. But Paul wouldn't have him . . . Tempers flared, and they ended up going their separate ways: Barnabas took Mark and sailed for Cyprus; Paul chose Silas and . . . went to Syria and Cilicia' (Acts 15:39–41, *The Message*).

Paul was not the only apostle to be locked in unresolved conflict. Peter suffered similarly. He found himself on the receiving end of the finger-pointing criticism that has crippled more than one Christian leader since.

Believing that he is acting in accordance with the will of God, Peter takes the unprecedented, unilateral decision to baptise Gentiles in the Name of Jesus. Luke recalls how swiftly the news travelled:

> In no time the leaders and friends back in Jerusalem heard about it – heard that the non-Jewish 'outsiders' were now 'in'. When Peter got back to Jerusalem, some of his old associates, concerned about circumcision, called him on the carpet: 'What do you think you're doing rubbing shoulders with that crowd, eating what is prohibited and ruining our good name?'
>
> (Acts 11:1ff, *The Message*)

Christians are still quarrelling among themselves. They always will. David Cormack puts it realistically: *'From the tranquillity of Eden's tree to the eternal peace of God's new city in Revelation lies a path of everlasting [unresolved] conflict.'*[1]

The source of unresolved conflict

Some Christians believe that the source of such conflict rests in Satan. After all, they argue, did he not cause Eve to fall in the first place and did he not tempt Jesus?

Satan is certainly the tempter par excellence. As Michael Green reminds us in *I Believe in Satan's Downfall*, Jesus

> has more to say about Satan than anyone else in the Bible. He has no doubt whatever of his reality. Satan is the one who tempted him so skilfully and fiercely, and who kept coming back at him with devious suggestions all through his ministry (Matt 4:1–11). It is the devil who snatches away the message of the good news from those who listen to it half-heartedly, or who sows tares in the field of God's wheat

(Mark 4:15, Matt 13:39). 'Deliver us from the evil one' is a crucial petition he taught his disciples to pray (Matt 6:13) . . . Jesus knows that the devil has usurped God's place of leadership in this world: it does lie in his hand to bestow 'all the kingdoms of the world and the glory of them' (Matt 4:8) and Jesus does not deny it. Rather than compromise with this subtle and evil force, Jesus knows that he must oppose him to the bitter end. Hence the way of the cross . . .[2]

As Michael Green goes on to insist, this is just a small part of the teaching of Jesus about Satan. There is more – much more – in the Gospels. The Gospels relate story after story of Jesus' face-to-face encounter with the father of lies himself. 'There is more in the Gospels about Satan than anywhere else in the Bible, as if the appearance of the Prince of heaven challenged the Prince of hell to frenzied activity.'[3]

Other Bible authors wax equally eloquent on the subject of Satan.

From Genesis to Revelation we are confronted by an anti-God force of great power and cunning. He is arrogant and determined, the implacable foe of God and man[kind], who is out to spoil and mar all that is good and lovely. We find him in the Garden of Eden at the beginning of the story. We find him in the lake of fire at the Bible's end. We find him tempting David, tempting Saul, tempting the Israelites, tempting Job.[4]

And we shall find him tempting us. There is no shred of doubt about that. I think of married couples for example. It is now a well-established fact that for at least a couple of decades, Satanists in the United Kingdom and elsewhere have been fasting and praying for the breakdown of Christian marriages. The catalogue of calamitous Christian marriages should not therefore surprise us, maybe?

Or I think of some of the countries that I have visited to provide pastoral care of Mission Partners. While living and working in certain areas, the sense of oppression is sometimes so tangible that it seems to envelop me in a thick, clammy, cloud-like substance. Only when I step off the plane in Cyprus where I live does the cloud appear to lift. The experience frequently reminds me of Paul's observation: *'Our fight is not against human foes, but against cosmic powers, against the authorities and potentates of this dark world, against the superhuman forces of evil in the heavens'* (Eph 6:12).

In the light of such awareness and the seeming success of the activity of Satan and his minions, we need to hold two things in balance. One is that, though Satan retains some power, he is not all powerful. He is the defeated foe. The other is that we need to heed the clear warning of Scripture – to be on our guard, ever watchful, ever prayerful. Satan takes an informed interest, not only in Christian marriages, but in other Christian relationships also. He schemes either to bring about their downfall or to pollute them. This is one of the reasons why seemingly unresolvable conflict frequently flares up and flows, like a river of fire, through resourceful relationships that are deeply embedded in God. We find many examples of such Satan-triggered conflict in the Bible.

Take Genesis 3, for example. Here we watch Satan sidle, snake-like, into the first marriage. Snakes hide and watch and wait before pouncing on their prey. They pounce only when the prey is vulnerable. Satan takes note of Eve's Achilles' heel. He succeeds in looting the happiness of the couple. Moreover, with skill and cunning, he sets them against each other so that they accuse and blame one another. Where nothing but harmony once existed, strife now prevails. Satan has not changed his tactics. They are old, yet somehow ever-new. If you are engaged to a Christian or married to one, if you live in a Christian household or community, if you work in a Christian partnership or team, if you work for God in a country where God's Name is not honoured or glorified or even if your contact with Christians is minimal, expect tension. Expect conflict – the kind of clashes and disharmony, incompatibility and fights for supremacy we listed at the beginning of this book. Satan, the trouble-maker, the father of lies, has you on his visiting list. He visits to disrupt and to destroy. The Bible has provided us with clear procedural instructions for such eventualities. Fight Satan, not fellow believers! As Eugene Peterson paraphrases Ephesians 6:12: embark on a 'life-or-death fight to the finish against the Devil and all his angels'. Resist the evil one: 'Yell a loud *no* to the Devil and watch him scamper' (Jas 4:7). 'Stand united' with fellow Christians (Phil 1:27). Pray (Eph 6:18). 'Prayer is essential in this ongoing warfare. Pray hard and long. Pray for your brothers and sisters. Keep your eyes open. Keep each other's spirits up so that no one falls behind or drops out.'

In other words, be on the alert and when the enemy strikes, take the initiative with the kind of boldness we take when silencing a barking but chained guard dog. As Paul promises, when Christians take authority over Satan in the name of Jesus, the enemy slinks away: a defeated, mangy lion. His power has been circumscribed by the victory Jesus won at Calvary. The Bible exhorts us to fix our eyes on Jesus, the author and finisher of our faith, not on Satan. Although he is ever-active, his power is limited.

Self-will: the taproot of unresolved conflict

Although Satan's power is limited, it is not non-existent. On the contrary, it is subtle and persistent. He knows where to strike to wound and to win.

One of his subtle ploys is to place the spotlight on himself; to encourage Christians in the belief that he is the source of *all* conflict. When disagreements flare up or Christians hurt one another, they are therefore quick to point the finger at the father of lies and blame him. This way they fail to acknowledge their own responsibility for the chaos caused, missing a golden opportunity to grow in grace and in handling relationships.

If we fail to acknowledge our own responsibility, we absolve ourselves from the unhelpful contribution we make to unresolved friction. We might even claim: 'It's not me, it's Satan.'

Geoff, whom I met at a conference for newly-weds with his wife, Sally, did just this. At the conference, their apparent love for one another was a delight to watch. Subsequently, though, they came to ask for help because Geoff's temper-tantrums were resulting in frightening outbursts of violence. He never imagined he would ever stoop to wife-beating and was desperate to break free from the web in which he appeared to be caught. At one stage, however, he insisted that the problem was somehow out of his control. 'Don't you think I'm possessed with a spirit of anger?' he would frequently ask. I have been in places and with people where, it would appear, a spirit of anger had a firm foothold; where deliverance ministry was clearly necessary. So far as I could discern, however, there was no evidence whatsoever of demon oppression or possession in Geoff's life. On the contrary, there was a great deal of evidence of blatant, innate selfishness: the self-centredness that lashes out, even at one's nearest and dearest, when it cannot have its own way. While Geoff insisted that a devilish agent was the cause of his violent outbursts, he demanded that *others* should do something about the problem: '*Deliver me from it*'. When, eventually, he saw that the root of the violence originated in his own person, he knew that he had some hard work to do to co-operate with the Holy

Spirit of God who is pledged to change us into the likeness of Christ.

It cannot therefore be underlined strongly enough that the taproot of unresolved conflict lies, not in Satan, but much nearer home – *in our own hearts*. James paints the picture powerfully:

Where do you think all these appalling wars and quarrels come from? Do you think they just happen? Think again. They come about because you want your own way, and fight for it deep inside yourselves. You lust for what you don't have and are willing to kill to get it. You want what isn't yours and will risk violence to get your hands on it . . . You wouldn't think of just asking God for it, would you? And why not? Because you know you'd be asking for what you have no right to. You're spoiled children, each wanting your own way.

(James 4:2ff, *The Message*)

James is simply building on an insistence underlined by Jesus: 'All of you listen . . . and try to understand . . . From *within* come evil thoughts . . . they are what pollute you' (Mark 7:14, 18, LB, emphasis mine).

How accurate these frightening observations are! Has anyone portrayed this more vividly and accurately than William Golding in *Lord of the Flies*. The best-selling novel reveals what happens when a group of young boys is suddenly marooned on a desert island. The film based on the book begins beautifully. Frightened, stripped of adult support, supervision and protection, the children demonstrate an impressive degree of resilience and initiative. They choose a leader and co-operate with him and with each other as they make contingency plans. They establish a workable, even an enjoyable and adventurous rhythm of life. They thrive. Gradually, though, beauty turns to nail-biting, heart-stopping horror. Values like communication, co-operation and unity evaporate like the morning mist. First one, then another, then yet another, challenge, criticise and abandon the appointed leader. They set up a rival gang. Trust patterns are dashed to pieces as they lie to one another, steal from one another and even try to kill one another. As the gang sinks deeper and deeper into uncontrolled and unbridled savagery, the voice of one of the boys echoes round the island. 'They even broke my glasses . . . They even broke my glasses.' Short-sighted in the extreme, this chubby, loyal, lovable lad is dependent on his spectacles. Without them he scarcely dares to take an unaided step forward. Knowing this, in one of their raids, the gang goes for the jugular. They trample on the glasses of the boy they believe to be a wimp. One of the lenses splinters and the arms break. 'They even broke my glasses . . . They even broke my glasses . . .' That pathetic complaint seemed to encapsulate the depths to which the youths had stooped.

The film, like the book, is deeply disturbing simply because it is so true to life that it shatters our complacency. Like children, adults can sink into similar depravity and degradation. We see this happening with monotonous regularity – even in the church. A pastor, for example, wants one kind of worship and the congregation another. Consequently, in the name of God, they quarrel and fight, crippling and wounding one another emotionally and spiritually in the process. At times some even use prayer as a weapon, using it to try to persuade God to ensure that they win the fight for supremacy over their opponent(s).

Or a congregation opposes a pastor's leadership style so they set out to challenge and criticise and, in effect, set up rival gangs. They spit abuse at one another, tear one another apart verbally, dispense with the thin veneer that hides their fallenness and conveniently forget James' injunction:

The tongue [is] only a tiny part of the body, but it can proudly claim that it does great things. Think how small a flame can set fire to a huge forest; the tongue is a flame like that. Among all the parts of the body, the tongue is a whole wicked world in itself: it infects the whole body; catching fire itself from hell, it sets fire to the whole wheel of creation . . . Nobody can tame the tongue – it is a pest that will not keep still, full of deadly poison. We use it to bless the Lord and Father, but we also use it to curse men who are made in God's image: the blessing and the curse come out of the same mouth. My brothers this must be wrong.

(James 3:5–10, JB)

Such destructive behaviour is not new, as we have observed. We first see it raising its ugly head in Genesis 3 when Satan sidled alongside Eve and appealed to that part of her that *wanted to be as God*. Ever since then, each daughter of Eve and every son of Adam, has been plagued with a similar temptation. We face a series of lifelong choices: to live life God's way or to manipulate circumstances so that life revolves around self.

Paul was particularly conscious of this inner turmoil and of those parts of our personality that lie hidden yet are far from inactive. He lumped them all together and referred to them as 'the old nature'. As we observed in chapter two, in a moving paragraph in his letter to the Romans, he acknowledges that the unregenerate and the regenerate parts of himself frequently fight each other:

I'm full of myself – after all, I've spent a long time in sin's prison. What I don't understand about myself is that I decide one way, but then I act another, doing things I absolutely despise . . . I decide to do good, but I don't *really* do it; I decide not to do bad, but then I do it anyway. My decisions, such as they

are, don't result in actions. *Something has gone wrong deep within me* and gets the better of me every time ... Is there no one who can do anything for me?
The answer, thank God, is that Jesus Christ can and does. He acted to set things right in this life of contradictions where I want to serve God with all my heart and mind, but am pulled by the influence of sin to do something totally different.

(Romans 7:15ff, *The Message*, my emphasis)

Twentieth-century Christians are in urgent need of becoming as self-aware as Paul seems to have been. We also need to acknowledge that we are full of ourselves, that we have spent a life-time in sin's prison, that something has gone wrong deep within us, that much of our failure in relationships resides in our own sin-pocked personality.

As David Cormack claims so memorably:

I need look no further than myself for the sources of conflict . . . Conflict is an outward manifestation of what I am inwardly . . . a self-centred, selfish being and when I meet another just like myself, then 'like poles repel'. . . In conflicts there are no 'innocent parties'. Both are guilty of attempting to pursue their own goals at the expense of the other. Both are faulty. There are no saints in the [unresolved] conflict business.[5]

In other words, the tree of our life is corrupt from the taproot up: through the trunk to each branch and twig and leaf. The tragedy is that we fail to acknowledge this. Instead of praying with Thomas Merton, 'deliver me from the prison of my self-hood', like the Pharisee in Jesus' parable of the Pharisee and the tax collector, in effect, we flesh out the Pharisee's prayer: 'Oh, God, I thank you that I am not like other people – robbers, crooks, adulterers . . .' (Luke 18:10ff, *The Message*).

The egocentricity of others

Because self-will lies at the root of sin and permeates every particle of every person who walks this earth, just as it is instinctive for me to live for number one, to feed my desires and demand my own way, so my husband, my children, my friends, my neighbours and the members of the church where I worship are tainted with the same instinct. We are each as egocentric as the other, expressing our desires equally fiercely and relentlessly. The result, as David Cormack points out is a seemingly-unbreakable cycle of clashes and quarrels: 'The normal rhythm of life is concord-conflict-concord-conflict-concord-conflict'.[6]

Even though the blood of Christ flows through our veins cleansing and healing, even though we may all be journeying along the pathway to sanctification, even though we have been rescued from the kingdom of darkness and brought into the Kingdom of God's Son (Col 1:13), we change, oh, so slowly. Paul seeks to persuade the Christians in Corinth of this vital fact: 'As the Spirit of the Lord works within us, we [gradually] become more and more like him' (2 Cor 3:18, LB). Even with the Spirit's aid, dying to the sin-biased self is a slow, long-drawn-out process. Meanwhile, we are rather like dying wasps – not only equipped to sting, but still capable of using that sting to wound. When someone presses on an open sore in my life, leaving me frightened or threatened or when someone offends me, I am not above retaliating. The dividing line between love and hate is wafer-thin. In fact, the claim is often made that love and hatred are two sides of the same coin.

I became all too aware of this two days before I began the original manuscript of *Conflict: Friend or Foe?* One minute David and I were sauntering along in the warm sunshine, hand in hand, contented companions; the next minute pain prised us apart. One minute we were as one as we stood drinking in the grandeur of the scenery: clear blue sky, snow-crowned mountains, pink and white almond blossom, pillar-straight pines; the next minute it was as though a chill cloud blanketed our world. Yet there was not a cloud in sight. Only the silent hostility between us spoiled the splendour of the day.

It was hot. David, my husband, wilts in warm weather. We wandered into a supermarket. 'Look! Ice-cold drinks in the fridge. I'm going to buy some.'

'But they're all *fizzy* drinks. You know I don't like fizzy stuff. Let's go on a bit. There's a café on top of that hill over there. I can smell the coffee. We could sit in the sun, have a drink and rest.'

'Coffee! Who wants coffee in this weather. Cold drinks are much better. Come on, let's buy some.'

I watched David choose a can of cool coke from the fridge, swallowed my anger, and stalked out of the supermarket in front of him – seething inwardly at this demonstration of seeming selfishness on his part. 'Can't he see that I have needs too?' I fumed inwardly.

'D'you want a sip of my coke? It's very nice.'

David's teasing burst in on my unexpressed bitterness. To his amazement I burst into tears leaving him wondering why my mood had swung so swiftly from contentment to resentment.

'Is everything all right? Have I done something wrong?'

By this time the emotions rising inside me were so strong I dared not speak. I stood, silent, sullen, sorrowful, gazing at the mountains and the almond blossom whose still splendour now seemed to mock me. Detached from David, I was detached from this magnificence also. All I wanted was a hole where I could take the seeming ugliness of my emotions, empty them out and hide until some sort of equilibrium could be established between us again. But we were overseas staying in a holiday apartment. I knew of nowhere to hide. So we drove in snow-cold silence, back to our tiny, temporary home, victims of unresolved conflict.

I remember that contest well for a number of reasons. One is that, when we reached our apartment, I did go off on my own to process my emotions in the way I described in chapter 2. As I did so, I found myself involuntarily working my way through a process I now call 'the Seven E's' because each part of the procedure begins with the letter E.

First I recalled and re-lived the *event*, reminding myself what, precisely, had caused the clash that now left me feeling bruised and battered. Next, I recorded my memories in my journal in the form of a letter to God. As I remembered and as I wrote, a jumble of *emotions* clamoured for attention. I *expressed* these in my journal: anger, bitterness, hatred, resentment, rejection, disappointment, fear, rejection, bleakness, blackness, sadness . . .

Listing the emotions felt rather like letting steam escape from a pressure cooker. Once the steam had gone, I could think rationally again – rationally enough to *evaluate* the feelings. God seemed to lead me into this phase by instructing me to turn to 1 Corinthians 13:4–7 and to place my emotions alongside the ingredients of love Paul lists there:

> Love is patient and kind
> Love is not jealous or conceited or proud
> Love is not ill-mannered or selfish or irritable
> Love does not keep a record of wrongs
> Love is not happy with evil
> Love is happy with the truth
> Love never gives up   (GNB)

I looked first at my list, next at Paul's list and then at another list drawn up by Paul – the jealousy, anger, ambition, divisiveness, envy, immorality, party-faction he mentions in Galatians 5:20 and the bitterness, hateful feelings, shouting and insulting he includes in Ephesians 4:31. As though with the impact of a revelation, I suddenly saw that Paul's ode to love is the very antithesis of Paul's other lists and much of my list. *These* lists are stark evidence of 'the compulsions of selfishness'; certain signs of the presence of the 'root of sinful self-interest' that is at odds with God's Spirit.[7] As such, many of my emotions, I realised, needed not to be harboured but to be confessed.

At that moment, I felt like giving up. I had recently re-read C.S. Lewis' *Screwtape Letters* though, so was quick to recognise the strategy of the *evil one*, the father of lies, who would persuade me that there was simply no point in trying to discern how the rift could promote the growth rather than the demise of our relationship. Having resisted him, I was free to focus on the pain that paralysed my heart and mind: the sense of sadness and rejection, bleakness and blackness I mentioned. As I *exposed* my innermost self to God, it was as though he came and held me. In this loved place, I found a prayer rising from my heart – not the question I had asked scores of times before: 'Lord, when are you going to change *David* so that our relationship can be sweeter?' but 'Lord, how do you want *me* to change so that our relationship can go on growing?'

As I prayed that prayer, a picture rose before my eyes: of a wood carver gazing at a piece of wood. Whereas most people would have seen nothing more than dead wood, the wood carver's practised, penetrating eye saw, instead, the graceful figurine that was hiding deep inside the 'deadness'. The mental visual aid reminded me that God's eyes similarly penetrate our failures and our griefs. They see the person he always created us to be. Conflict, I suddenly saw, can be like a chisel that the skilled hand of God uses to whittle away all that obscures and mars the image of his indwelling Son. The chisel will not disfigure us but rather set us free to become the person God created us to be. But he rarely hurries. I must therefore *exercise patience* and trust that when conflict and other tools have chipped away all that is un-Christlike, our lives and our marriage will gradually become 'brighter and more beautiful as . . . we become like him' (2 Cor 3:18, *The Message*).

I wanted this freedom and I wanted this growth so, with a sense of relief and penitence, I asked God to cleanse me from *my* contribution to the quarrel. And, of course, he did!

Now that I had processed my feelings, some words of Jesus made such perfect sense to me that I *wanted* to go to David to apologise for my childish, selfish outburst in the mountains. The words of Jesus were these:

'Why do you look at the speck of sawdust in your brother's eye and pay no attention to the plank in your own eye? How can you say to your brother, "Let me take the speck out of your eye," when all the time there is a plank in your own eye? You hypocrite, first take the plank out of your own eye, and then you will see clearly to remove the speck from your brother's eye.'

(Matt 7:3–5)

Another reason why I remember this particular collision so well is that, because of it, I became acutely aware that, when pain pushes people apart, the repercussions on their lives are many, varied and serious. Our inner peace is disrupted for one thing and, as we saw in chapter two, this has serious consequences for our relationships as well as our well-being. Our attitudes may become poisoned for another and this, in turn, saps our energy, deflates us and erects a barrier between ourselves and God. Life then becomes so stressful that we lose hope, lose sleep and recoil from the person with whom we have clashed or quarrelled or collided.

Yet another reason why I remember this seemingly trivial incident so vividly is that my whole being was crying out: 'I don't want our relationship to be like this. It's not the way God intended it to be.' At the same time, I realised that, in very many ways, we had brought this grievous gulf that now separated us upon ourselves. Let me explain.

The disagreement took place a few days after our much-longed-for sabbatical leave had started. When I came face to face with my own selfishness and asked myself the question: 'How could self possibly gain the upper hand over something as inconsequential as a can of Coca-Cola?', I realised that the question of the drink was simply the peg on which we were hanging the frustration of months.

We had been over-working; sacrificing our marital relationship on the altar of the parish work in which we were both engaged at that time: counselling, preaching, teaching, writing, befriending, giving hospitality. We were well aware that busyness was siphoning off vital energy from our relationship: spiritual, sexual and emotional. We were depriving each other of the time, attention and cherishing on which zestful marriages thrive. Because of various crises in the parish, and because the end was in sight, we had been willing to allow this to continue. 'We'll sort that out when we're on sabbatical' was a resolve that had become a cliché.

Now the much-longed-for sabbatical was hours old. What was being expressed through the backbiting over a drink was the impatience we both felt as we waited for the resurgence of free-flowing love that comes with relaxation and deeply shared lives. What was also being expressed, albeit subconsciously, was the accumulation of months of unresolved tension and unmet needs. We had not discovered in those days that to deprive one another of very basic needs has the same effect as watering the roots of a plant. We failed to discern that we were faithfully watering the taproot of self-centredness that thrives in both of us.

A month later, after we had unwound together, revised the art of relaxing together, studied and prayed together, that quarrel could not have flared up. By then we had rediscovered the joy of being sensitive to the other's needs; relearned the miracle-working power of gentleness, begun to thank God from the depths of our hearts for the mutuality of the friendship we still enjoy. By then we were able to nod wisely, even to smile at the truth of the following claims: 'We should expect each other to be sinful, unpleasant at times and difficult to live with . . . If we expect perfection from others . . . we will only succeed in being unable to appreciate anything that anyone does. To expect perfection from any but God is to crush them.'[8]

Suggested exercises

The taproot of self-will inevitably gives birth to shoots of self-centredness and self-absorption. Our task in the next chapter will be to place the spotlight on some of the manifestations of such shoots. Meanwhile, rather than rush onto that chapter, you might prefer to pause and act on the following:

1. Think of occasions when, in the past week, you have, in effect, prayed the prayer of the Pharisee: 'God, I thank you that I am not like other members of my family, that member of my house group that is so obnoxious, those people in church . . .'
Ask God to remind you of such occasions. Talk to God about your hypocrisy and self-absorption.

2. Think of recent occasions when those near and dear to you have acted in an uncharacteristically *unselfish* way. Perhaps they have been more gentle than usual or more sensitive or more discerning. Marvel at this sign that God's Spirit is at work in them. Thank them if this seems appropriate. Pray

for them.

3. Think of a conflict situation in which you are currently locked if there is one. Work your way through the Seven E's I have sketched in this chapter and that are described in greater detail on p 184ff. See if this method of processing inner turmoil works for you.

4. Ask yourself, 'How do *I* feel when there is a rift between myself and a loved one, a colleague, a neighbour or a member of the fellowship?

5. Think of occasions when you have been very conscious of the speck in another person's eye while remaining oblivious to the plank in your own eye. Talk to God about it. Let God speak to you.

6. Pray for yourself using this prayer if you can do so with integrity:
   Lord, deliver me from the prison of my self-hood.
   Turn my whole being to your praise and glory.

7. If you can, do what Neville Ward challenges us to do when he insists that we must forgive earth for not being heaven. Read David Runcorn's reflection on that phrase. Notice and perhaps record your reactions to it or write your own version of it:

I Forgive

I forgive   earth for not being he..
time for not being etern..
earth for not being certain.
dust for not being glory.

I forgive   beginnings for not being ending.
questions for not being answers
confusion for not being understandi..
darkness for not being light

I forgive   mind for not being heart
man for not being woman
passion for not being love
conflict for not being peace
evil for not being good

you for not being me

I forgive

and holding a mirror to the prayer
I start again

I forgive forgiveness never ending.[9]

4

SOME SHOOTS OF SELFISHNESS

oot, I am a self-centred, self-willed, self-absorbed, self-worshipping person whose determination to hold the reins of my own life is fierce. When I encounter others whose life similarly revolves around self (that is, to varying degrees, anyone and everyone who walks this earth), clashes are almost inevitable. That's the nub of chapter 3 in which we likened our lives to a tree whose taproot is diseased.[1] Roots give birth to shoots. Our task in this chapter is to observe some of the shoots that spring from the taproot of self-absorption. Such shoots are subtle – scarcely discernible until we search for them. One is the selfishness that permeates almost all of the hopes and expectations we bring to bear on relationships. When we stop to analyse such hopes and expectations, they almost always beg the question: *'What's in it for me?'* rather than or at best as well as: *'How will this benefit the other(s)?'* or *'How will this further the Kingdom of God?'*.

Unrealistic demands

When couples marry, for example, their unexpressed hopes often conceal this seam of self-centredness. Lawrence Crabb makes this point well in *Marriage Builder* when he surmises what might be in the mind of couples on their wedding day:

> Consider what may really be happening when a couple get married: Two people, each with personal

needs pressing for fulfilment, pledge themselves to become one. As they recite their vows to love and respect each other, strong but hidden motivations stir inside them. If a tape recorder could somehow tune into the couple's unconscious intentions, I wonder if perhaps we would hear words like these:

Bridegroom: I need to feel important and I expect you to meet that need by submitting to my every decision, whether good or bad; by respecting me no matter how I behave; and by supporting me in whatever I choose to do. I want you to treat me as the most important man in the world. My goal in marrying you is to find my significance through you. An arrangement in which you are commanded by God to submit to me sounds very attractive.

Bride: I have never felt as deeply loved as my nature requires. I am expecting you to meet that need through gentle affection even when I'm growling. [I am also expecting you to give me] thoughtful consideration whether I am always sensitive to you or not, and an accepting, romantic sensitivity to my emotional ups and downs. Don't let me down.[2]

Each bride and every bridegroom will harbour their own variation of such hidden hopes and longings. Perhaps neither realises at this stage that, though they claim to love *one another*, these unexpressed expectations reveal that each loves self more than the other. Both are concerned, not primarily with the question, '*How can I make my partner happy?*' but rather, '*How can my partner make me happy?*' Both desire intimacy but neither has yet realised that intimacy carries a high price tag: what Carl Jung described as an invasion of the individual ego that each person resists until the ego has developed an acceptable level of tolerance. When a husband and wife set out to become one – more and more involved in each other's lives, socially, sexually, spiritually, intellectually, emotionally, they instinctively, but surreptitiously, erect barriers that will prevent the other encroaching deeper into the sanctuary of their innermost emotional and spiritual being than they feel comfortable with. Gradually, given time and a great deal of sensitivity, one or other or both will lower their defences ever so little until, in the healthiest and most intimate of unions, the boundaries are removed for at least part of most days. But this growth in intimacy takes time, patience, and a great deal of understanding love.

Mike Mason describes this bitter-sweet process with heart-warming honesty:

> No one has ever been married without being shocked at . . . the monstrous inconvenience of this thing called intimacy which suddenly invades their life. At the wedding a bride and groom may have gone through the motions of the candlelighting ceremony, each blowing out their own flame and lighting one central candle in place of the two, but the touching simplicity of this ritual has little in common with the actual day-to-day pressures involved as two persons are merged into one. It is a different matter when the flame that must be extinguished is no lambent flicker of a candle, but the blistering inferno of self-will and independence. There is really nothing else like this lifelong cauterization of the ego that must take place in marriage. All of life is, in one way or another, humbling. But there is nothing like the experience of being humbled by another person, and by the same person day in and day out. It can be exhausting, unnerving, infuriating, disintegrating. There is no suffering like the suffering involved in being close to another person. But neither is there any joy nor any real comfort at all outside of intimacy, outside the joy and the comfort that are wrung out like wine from the crush and ferment of two lives being pressed together.[3]

'There is no suffering like the suffering involved in being close to another person.' There is no indignity like the indignity of this cauterisation of the ego. There is no pain like the pain of being crushed in the wine-press of intimacy. For intimacy breeds friction. You cannot have one without the other. The closer two people become, the more they experience the oneness that was God's intention for married people, the more they open themselves to the possibility of clashes of personality, preferences, options, habits. This is inevitable. After all, in marriage, they are attempting to fuse two imperfect, self-oriented persons – so to unite two imperfects that they become one flesh.

In generations past, when 'traditional marriages' were the norm, both husband and wife brought very different expectations to their relationship from today's bride and groom. In traditional marriages, the husband's breadwinning role took him out of the home all day while his wife's homemaking, child-rearing role tied her to the house. In traditional marriages, if both partners fulfilled their roles with reasonable efficiency, the marriage was applauded: 'good', even 'successful' were the terms used to describe it. If intimacy and companionship grew up between the spouses, that was an uninvited bonus, a perk for which both partners were gratefully surprised. Such mutuality was not a prerequisite for a happy marriage.

Today all that has changed. Couples have stripped off the concept of traditional marriage in the same way as they discard unfashionable clothing. They marry, not to fulfil a role, but for companionship, for mutuality, for the giving and receiving of happiness and love. Their expectations of the marital relationship are high. Without realising it, they have pushed wide open the door to the clashes that are part and parcel of closeness.

Unrealistic expectations

Married people are not the only ones to approach relationships with secret, selfish expectations. My mind goes, for example, to Paul and Anne.[4] Paul was a successful young executive when he sensed he heard God asking him to train to work in the church. He and Anne, his wife, prayed long and hard before giving up their comfortable home and their financial security to sacrifice them on the altar of 'the full-time ministry'. Since the call seemed so clear, however, they knew they must obey, whatever the cost to themselves or their children.

After two years of training, Paul and Anne emerged from college, full of zeal and counting it a privilege to be embarking on ministry together. They had visited the church where they were to work and were delighted to find that they related well to the pastor and his wife. They had also met and appreciated key members of the congregation. Their expectations soared. The pastor, his wife and their family would model to them what an ideal Christian family in leadership was intended to be. They would pray together as a foursome and forge ahead as a team for the extension of God's kingdom. Of course, these expectations were never committed to words. Paul and Anne simply assumed that Jeremy and his wife, like every other minister in the country (so Paul and Anne supposed), would share their ideals. They seemed so basic, so natural, so right to Paul and to Anne.

After they had settled into their new home and the first-blush euphoria of early-ministry days had evaporated, they began to hear whispers about the pastor's teenagers. Words like rude, rebellious, standoffish were used to describe them. While they were still recoiling from this shock, Jeremy's wife dropped another bombshell. For a variety of reasons – both financial and emotional – she had decided to take a full-time job. 'I really need to discover myself again after years of being buried under children, nappies and church work.' What had happened? Where had they gone wrong? Paul and Anne's cherished biblical model of the pastor's family lay at their feet like pieces of cracked and broken pottery and the pastor's wife seemed intent on servicing *herself* rather than her family or the church. This meant, of course, that Jeremy's wife would not journey alongside Paul and Anne in ministry, nor would she be available for supportive prayer and pastoring as they had hoped.

But Paul and Anne were resilient, optimistic, prayerful people. God had called them to work in this church. They were all Christians, so of course the relationship with Jeremy and his wife would eventually fall into place. Or so they assumed.

A year later, their dreams had crumbled and disillusionment had set in like leaden rain clouds. When I met them, they were all too ready to pour out their bewilderment and frustration. After a year of working as colleagues, Jeremy and Paul were locked in unresolved and seemingly unresolvable conflict; a collision that was sending ripples running through the entire church, reaching the people sitting in the hard pews every Sunday, and threatening to split the church in two: the pro-Jeremy's and the pro-Paul's.

As I listened to the catalogue of complaints Paul and Anne had compiled ('Jeremy is authoritarian rather than authoritative . . . He never listens when I make suggestions . . . We never meet for prayer and rarely see them as a family. Apart from Paul meeting with Jeremy there's a non-relationship. It's so sad. There's so much potential in the area round the church and Jeremy's not tapping it, nor even attempting to meet the needs of the congregation and so on and so on . . .) I found a question formulating in my mind: 'What hurts you most about this sad saga?' I was interested to discover that it wasn't that Jeremy was failing to nur-

ture the congregation. Nor was it that he was failing to
evangelise the neighbourhood. What was hurting Paul
and Anne most was that their own initial hopes and
expectations had never been met. They had never been
met because they had never been spelled out. If, before
they had become colleagues, Paul and Anne had said
that they expected support and prayer and pastoring
and personal care and if they had spelled out the hope
that Jeremy's family would be a role model for their
own family, maybe Jeremy and his wife could have
pricked the bubble of expectation right from the very
beginning. Maybe they might even have made themselves vulnerable and confessed that they were struggling. Maybe they might have revealed the truth – that
Jeremy's wife was in turmoil. She was working her
way through a tempestuous mid-life crisis and suffering from menopausal depression as a consequence. To
make matters worse, their teenagers were kicking over
the traces: working their way through the triumphs
and traumas of the teen years. The consequent turbulence was disrupting the entire family dynamic. They
had no intention of rejecting their new colleagues yet it
was the sting of perceived rejection that most plagued
Paul and Anne when they spoke to me.

Arrogant attitudes and assumptions

Paul and Anne's perceived rejection gave rise to a torrent of criticism as we have seen. As I listened to them,
I tuned into the pain rather than the bitterness.
Consequently, I found myself hurting for both couples.
If Paul and Anne were here with me today, now that I
have had years to reflect on the situation, I might *gently* ask them a series of questions – like:

'Has it ever occurred to you that you accepted this
job assuming that Jeremy and his wife would serve
you? Did it ever occur to you to ask, "How can we
serve them?" Has it ever occurred to you that they have

rights too? Has it ever occurred to you that you seem to be assuming that Jeremy and his wife should be like you in their prayer preferences and their behaviour patterns? Might it be possible that your hidden hopes and unexpressed expectations were, in effect, self-centred demands? Is it possible that the taproot of self-absorption has given birth in you to the shoot of pride?'

The reason why I might ask these questions is that, over the years, as I have observed conflicts of varying kinds, been embroiled in conflict of varying kinds and counselled those who have been caught in conflict's crossfire, I have noted how frequently the root of self-love on which we placed the spotlight in chapter 3 gives birth to the shoot of pride.

Pride, as Esther de Waal defines it, 'is the desire to control, to control my day, my future, the other people in my life, to make sure that the world is put together the way I want it'.[5]

Pride can make arrogant assumptions – like, 'everyone should think and behave like me'. Pride can also harbour arrogant attitudes – like, anyone who does not think and behave like me and anyone who does not share my preferences, my theological viewpoint or my tastes must be flawed in some way. My God-given role in life includes challenging, correcting and changing these flaws. We might not spell out our mission in such blunt and blatant terms, but that is the goal towards which we constantly move. Our aim might be as seemingly innocent as to change the way someone else washes up or as profound and far-reaching as to challenge the way others do or don't pray. Whether at the sublime or the ridiculous end of the scale, we fail to see that we are pouring ourselves into Mission Undesirable! As authors Kiersey and Bates remind us: 'Our attempts to change spouse, offspring or others *can* result in a change, but the result is a scar and not a transformation.'[6] '*Remove the fangs of a lion and behold a toothless lion, not a domestic cat.*'[7] It follows that there is an urgent need to recognise differences for what they are – differences and not flaws.

People, including Christians, differ in fundamental ways. 'They *want* different things; they have different motives, purposes, aims, values, needs, drives, impulses, urges . . . They believe differently; they think, conceptualize, perceive, understand, comprehend differently.'[8] These differences in attitude, behaviour and preference may be variously explained – in terms of temperament or psychological type, for example, or in terms of age, spiritual growth, culture or race. The impact these differences make, not only to marriages and friendships, but to team life also, cannot and must not be underestimated.

Different personality preferences

Take personality differences, for example. My husband and I were almost forced into appraising these when we were members of a certain church team. The team was made up of three couples. We all believed God had called us to work together and rejoiced as we imagined what we, collectively, might achieve for God's Kingdom. To our dismay, however, slowly but surely, with the relentlessness of an incoming tide on a stormy day, tension crept into one relationship after another within the group. Soon it became patently clear that urgent action must be taken. We prayed, we talked, we socialised and we prayed some more. The situation grew steadily worse. We called in a professional counsellor who met with us two or three times. The situation deteriorated even further – until another counsellor, Tony, came to our rescue. He simply set himself the task of exploring with us the kind of personality preferences we were attempting to cream together. In order to do this, we arranged a time when it would be convenient for all of us to meet. By inviting everyone to respond to a confidential, written questionnaire, Tony would try to establish how each person was energised, how they perceived the world in which we live, how they coped with decision-making, in short what their personality preference or personality profiles were. He would not be trying to pigeonhole any of us but rather would seek to help us to understand ourselves, one another and some of the reasons why the ingredients we brought to the group curdled.

The meeting was duly arranged, and, on the designated day, we met in our home. Was the room in which we met filled with apprehension that bright and sunny morning, or was the fear only mine: the fear that asked questions like: 'Will I be hurt yet again?', 'Is it all my fault?' 'Can the situation ever improve?' 'Will Tony expose and despise secret failures and weaknesses?' Pride frequently produces fears like these. They mounted in me while Tony analysed the questionnaires that we had duly completed. In this instance, as it happened, such fears were groundless.

I shall never forget Tony's ice-breaking question nor the kind but somewhat mischievous twinkle in his eye when he asked: *'Whose bright idea was it to put the six of **you** together?'* Before anyone could answer, he asked another question: *'**How long** have you been working together?'* When he heard the reply, 'Two years', he shot yet another question across our bows: *'**How** have you managed to stick it for so long?!'*

The tension broke. We laughed together for the first time in well over a year as we chorused: 'With difficulty!' Tony went on to confess that he really admired us for attempting to work together for so long. The amazement and relief that filled the room was almost tangible. The clawing sense of guilt that had clung to us for so long dropped away almost visibly. Tony spent the rest of the day divulging why, in his view, we had been attempting Mission Impossible.

Extraverts and introverts

Three members of the group were extraverts, two of them extreme extraverts. Three were introverts – two of them extreme. Problem number one was rooted right here.

Extraverts thrive on being in the thick of things. They are re-energised by interaction with people and the muchness and manyness of activity. Their energy level drops dramatically when they are alone for long periods of time or when they lack social interaction so they never seem to mind but rather welcome telephone calls and unexpected visitors. When it comes to working at a project, the result of that task is what interests them. Long, slow, drawn-out projects therefore frustrate and irritate them and are likely to be left unfinished.

When they are involved in discussions or communication in general, extraverts are rarely stuck for words. In fact, there is more than a grain of truth in the claim that extraverts need to talk in order to discover what they are thinking. 'How do I know what is in my mind unless I hear myself saying it?' some extraverts have been heard to ask. Extraverts enjoy making relationships and make them easily, even effortlessly. Affirmation, encouragement and appreciation flow from their lips in rather the same way as water cascades from a waterfall.

Introverts, on the other hand, are re-energised by time alone, time to reflect, time to have their inner resources topped up. 'The unreflected life is no life at all,' they sigh. Whereas their extravert counterpart looks at life broadly, the introvert is not so much concerned with *breadth* as with *depth*. Introverts' energy levels are rapidly depleted by a barrage of ceaseless chatter. They function best when they can operate from a still centre – that is, when they are given uninterrupted time to reflect. During such time it is as though they are refreshed by hidden, life-giving wellsprings.

Conversely, if they are forced to do things in a hurry, they can become agitated and make stupid mistakes. As one introvert once put it to me, 'When I'm hassled, it's rather like rushing into a supermarket when there's no time to spare. You grab what you think you need only to discover later that you grabbed the wrong thing.'

Without quietness, introverts cannot concentrate. An interruption, like a telephone call, or someone popping their head round the door 'just to say "Hi!" ' can cut right across their train of thought and threaten, even ruin, a whole morning's work. They think carefully before they act – sometimes so carefully that the action never happens. They also ponder carefully before expressing an opinion. 'How can I comment until I've had time to reflect?' they complain when pounced on for a response. In a group situation, they may refrain from making any contribution unless they are invited. In a team situation, they can feel so overwhelmed by the cut and thrust of the chatter, the laughter and the camaraderie of their extravert counterparts that they feel strangely lonely, isolated, rejected and of little worth.

Insights like these came to many members of the group with the force of a revelation. They had never heard them before. But there was more.

To complicate matters further, four members of the group loved precision, order, structure, schedules, neatness, predictability, dependability, punctuality. The other two approached life in a far less structured way. They were the spontaneous types who dislike plans and organisers and decision-making; people who prefer to go with life's flow. For one, in particular, a deadline signified the time to *start* a project rather than the time to complete it – an attitude that was anathema to the two people with whom he worked most closely.

Thinkers and feelers

Further complications revealed themselves in that one member of the group was a 'thinker' – that is, his approach to life and, in particular, to decision-making was analytical, objective, seemingly detached from some of the painful pastoral problems church teams sometimes have to wrestle with. Like most 'thinkers', in the opinion of some members of the group, he sometimes expressed himself in a blunt, uncompromising way because, to him, choices seemed so obvious, so clear-cut. When faced with a complex question or a dilemma, he would approach it logically, prayerfully, thoroughly and apply to it his understanding of relevant biblical principles. At the end of such thorough research, reflection and prayer, his opinions had been firmly formed. He would then express this distilled wisdom with clarity, conviction and quiet authority. To 'feelers', the clear, crisp, crystallised deliberations of 'thinkers' can sound cold, clinical and uncaring. When faced with decisions of a sensitive pastoral nature like, should divorcees be allowed to marry again in church, 'feelers' are concerned, not so much with principles or even   theology but with an all-consuming concern about the effect the ultimate decision will have on the people concerned. The depth of this care for others can strengthen the shoot of pride that thrives in us all and produces an arrogant attitude. 'Why can't they see that people's lives are at stake here? We are not simply "talking theology". We're pontificating about flesh and blood people who worship with us, trust us and love us.' Equally that same shoot of pride in the 'thinker' can be fed by listening to the 'feeler's' protest and responding with the arrogant criticism that claims: 'You have to be objective. The Bible clearly says . . . ' The assumption is, of course, that their interpretation of, to them, key verses is the only one – the right one.

As one of the 'feelers' in our team, I remember how confused I sometimes became when listening to our 'thinker'. In my heart of hearts, I knew that he was *not* a cold, calculating, heartless person. I knew him to be a person of compassion – thoughtful, deeply caring. Then why was this so often camouflaged in meetings, I wondered.

The 'thinker' in the team was also the kind of person who gathers information through his senses. Such people are observant, factual, practical and realistic. In discussion, they demand facts and details and, when making plans, insist on having every step prepared in detail so that the various stages of a project can be articulated and minuted. Another member of the group was equally attentive to detail. The group's visionaries, the intuitive types who could dream a dream a minute but who seemed totally incapable of conjuring up ways of implementing plans, found their colleagues' down-to-earth questions like: 'How long do you think this will take?' or 'How many chairs do you think we'll need?' too irritating for words.

Almost any healthy group or team will consist of people who love precision and order and conversely, the spontaneous types who like to 'go with the flow'. Almost all healthy teams will also bring together a combination of 'thinkers' and 'feelers', extraverts and introverts, sensing people and intuitives, and many other combinations of personality preferences. People working in teams, as, indeed, people worshipping in the pews, need therefore to watch their attitudes and assumptions lest they display signs of arrogance. Just as it is easy for the 'feeler' to roar and boil inwardly like an angry sea and to assume that 'thinkers' are too black and white, so it is easy for the 'thinker' to look down their noses at 'feelers' and to assume that they overindulge their emotions; that feelings (their own and others) are estimated more highly than objectivity, commonsense and even God's Word. Just as it is easy for introverts to dismiss extraverts, complaining: 'They're so brash, so shallow, so thoughtless, so restless, so demanding, so draining to be with,' so it is easy for extraverts to accuse introverts of being unfriendly, stand-offish, aloof, hard to get to know, non-participatory members of group discussions. Just as it is easy for intuitives to accuse sensing people of being pernickity, so it is easy for sensing types to insist that intuitives are too dreamy, 'so heavenly minded that they are of no earthly use'.

Members of countless healthy teams glory in such differences, see them as a challenge, an opportunity to create harmony instead of cacophony and to offer a roundedness of ministry no one person could possibly offer. For several reasons, our team failed to approach our differences in this creative, positive way. We wanted to but we failed. One reason was that the majority of us were 'feelers'. 'Feelers' are deeply and adversely affected by anything that smacks of disunity and disharmony. Criticism crushes them leaving them emotionally crippled and unable to function efficiently. And they avoid conflict in rather the same way as pregnant women avoid catching measles. So the seemingly never-ending, unresolved conflict was paralysing most of us.

Another factor that mitigated against our oneness was that, as the conflict escalated, so each person's stress level rose. When we are stressed, our personality preferences become more marked, even exaggerated. Hence the gulf that already separated us gradually yawned wider and wider.

Men and women
Another reason why we allowed our differences to polarise us rather than to enrich us was that we were effectively a two-tiered team – a team within a team. The 'ministry team' proper consisted of the three men: my extravert husband who was the Rector, his introvert colleague, the vicar, who was the thinker and the extravert administrator whose impeccable concern for

detail equalled if not surpassed that of the vicar. To make matters even more delicate, my husband and the vicar were personality opposites. They could not have been more different. My husband's temperament (and that of others like him), is sometimes summarised in this way: 'Warmly enthusiastic, high-spirited, ingenious, imaginative, able to do almost anything that interests them. Quick with a solution for any difficulty and ready to help anyone with a problem. Often rely on their ability to improvise instead of preparing in advance. Can usually find compelling reasons for whatever they want.'

Conversely, our vicar's personality profile (and that of others like him) has been summarised in this way: 'Serious, quiet, earn success by concentration and thoroughness. Practical, orderly, matter-of-fact, logical, realistic and dependable. See to it that everything is well organized. Take responsibility. Make up their own minds as to what should be accomplished and work toward it steadily, regardless of protests or distractions'.[9]

In a perfect world, such complete opposites could supplement and complement each other, of course. In a perfect world two people approaching a certain situation from such opposite angles could each spot aspects of the task in hand that remain a mystery to the other. In our imperfect world, however, fallen human nature is such that two opposites like this rarely accept one another's point of view. They bring so many differences to the relationship that the individuals concerned may find it virtually impossible to work together harmoniously and creatively – particularly when one is a precise person who likes to bring things to a closure and the other is the happy-go-lucky, fun-loving kind of person who leaves things open ended. That is why it is now widely recognised that the best teamwork (even among Christians) is usually achieved by individuals who differ on one or two personality preferences only.

They then have some common preferences that will enable them to establish a basis of understanding, shared vision and ways of implementing their vision.

As though things were not fragile enough already, we added to the mix of men those shadowy, complex, but powerful people who formed the second tier of the team, we wives. We had no role of our own within this group. The six of us simply met for fellow-ship(!) and, from time to time, to act as a sounding board for our husbands. Like it or not, we brought to the group our own personal emotional baggage *and* certain hidden agendas: the perception of the mounting disharmony we had each received through our husband's filter and hurt.

Add just one other ingredient to the recipe, namely, the marriage dynamic of each couple and, with the wisdom of hindsight, it is not difficult to see why the recipe proved a disaster. One couple consisted of two introverts. Another couple consisted of two extraverts. The third was a 'mixed marriage' in that one partner was an extreme extravert while the other was an equally extreme introvert. No wonder the team's ingredients curdled.

Yet, as I write, I realise that my affection for each member of that team still runs deep. In a curious way, though we hurt one another by blaming one another, criticising one another, exasperating one another, draining one another, even believing we had no need of one another, we belonged to each other and still belong to one another. When we last met one of the couples concerned, just a few months before I started to write this book, we all marvelled at the way God has changed each of us. Although if we again attempted to work together in a team, we would still have to work hard at dove-tailing the particular mixture of personality preferences and gifting that is part and parcel of each person, we have all grown in understanding of ourselves, of one another, of the complexity of the situation and of human nature. Now, we can understand each other, relax with one another, be real with one another, be vulnerable with each other, express care for each other. Now we all adhere to Paul's conviction that we need each other:

> Suppose the whole body were an eye – then how would you hear? Or if your whole body were just one big ear, how could you smell anything?
> But that isn't the way God has made us. He has made many parts for our bodies and has put each part just where he wants it . . . The eye can never say to the hand, 'I don't need you.' The head can't say to the feet, 'I don't need you.' . . . *All of you together are the one body of Christ and each one of you is a separate and necessary part of it.*
> (1 Cor 12:17–23a, 27, LB, emphasis mine)

In fact, if we were to work together again, we could write our own parody on Paul's parable that might read something like this:

Suppose the whole body were a 'thinker' – who, then, would show compassion? Or if the whole body were just one big 'feeler', how could it ever behave rationally? Suppose the whole body were an intuitive? Who would book the hall, or arrange the chairs or make the tea? Or if the body was one big sensing person, who would give it vision? Suppose the whole body were an extravert? How would it ever heed God's command to be **still**? Or if the body were one big introvert, who would go out to welcome and befriend people and help them feel at home? All of us **together** are the one body of Christ.

Yes. With the wisdom of hindsight, we now acknowledge that it is arrogant for any of us to act as though we have no need of one another. Such attitudes and assumptions are not only arrogant, they feed and nurture pride. All of us together are the body of Christ.

Each of us is a separate, necessary and integral part of it.

An exercise for introverts and extraverts:

Having dwelt at length on the part personality preferences sometimes play in the eruption of conflict, our task in the next chapter will be to focus, among other things, on generation differences. Before reading on, however, maybe there would be value in pausing again and asking yourself:

Have there been times in my life when I've brought unrealistic hopes and expectations to a situation or relationship? If so, how do I view those demands in retrospect?

If you are an introvert, reflect on that question on your own or respond to it in your journal.

If you are an extravert, discuss the question with a few friends or with your house group.

You might like to add specific questions to that general one concentrating first on the fellowship to which you belong:
  • What am I expecting from the fellowship group to which I belong?
  • What can I give to it?
  • Are my expectations realistic?
  • What is it about me that needs to change so that my relationship with the fellowship can improve?
  • Is there something *in me* that is disrupting the unity of God's people?

Examine your response to these questions with care. If necessary, ask God to give you the grace to repent, that is, to turn your back on selfish behaviour and to determine to live differently. Ask the Holy Spirit to fill you and to impregnate you with his love for each person in the fellowship – particularly those you would not normally fraternise with.

Next focus on specific friendships that have been important to you in the past and that have disintegrated. Or focus on friendships that trouble you now:
- What was/is your expectation of this particular friendship?
- How realistic were/are those expectations?
- Were/are those expectations self-centred or other-oriented?
- How did/do they compare with your friend's hopes?
- If they are different, how would you describe the differences?
- Are there certain hopes and expectations that now need to be relinquished – either because they are unattainable or because God seems to be asking you to re-negotiate the friendship on a new set of terms?
- If a change seems imminent, how do you feel about the re-shaping of this particular relationship?
- How do you intend to act on the insights God seems to have given you?
- Does anything prevent you from holding this friendship on an open palm rather than in a clenched fist? In other words, are you and your friend free – to continue to relate closely or to let one another go?

Letting go of cherished hopes, expectations and relationships is rarely easy. It involves loss, disappointment, a sense of bereavement. When faced with the challenge to let go or to re-phrase friendships, it can be helpful to recall the Dynamic Cycle of Being and Well-Being – to practise doing what Jesus did: taking our pain, our emptiness, our loneliness, our hurt to God so

that we experience his perfect friendship and love.
   Look back at that Cycle on p 41.

Spend some time in quiet receiving God's accepting
love and sustenance. At the end of your time of quiet,
respond to the above questions again.

Finally, re-read and reflect on the definition of pride
that appears on p 87. Ask God, those close to you and
maybe even those with whom you work or study,
where pride raises its ugly little head in your life. Beg
God to deliver you from the prison of your self-hood.

5

Some Sour Fruit:
Hatred and Jealousy

Unresolved conflict is rooted in self-centredness. The root of self-centredness produces prolific and virulent shoots: shoots of pride, arrogance and fear. Such shoots, in turn and in time, produce crops of sour fruit. Paul names some of them: 'hatred and fighting, jealousy and anger, constant effort to get the best for yourself, complaints and criticisms, the feeling that everyone else is wrong except those in your own little group' (Gal 5:20ff, LB). Or, as Eugene Peterson paraphrases certain parts of that section of Paul's letter to the Galatians:

> It is obvious what kind of life develops out of trying to get your own way all the time: cut-throat competition; all-consuming-yet-never-satisfied wants; a brutal temper; an impotence to love or be loved; divided homes and divided lives; small-minded and lopsided pursuits; the vicious habit of depersonalizing everyone into a rival; uncontrolled and uncontrollable addictions . . . I could go on. (*The Message*)

'*I could go on . . .* ', writes Paul. In other words, there are other kinds of diseased fruit. Our task in this chapter is to name a few more kinds. I mentioned some in the last chapter when I described the personality clashes that had disrupted a team in which my husband and I were once involved. As I recorded the memories of that period of our life, I wept – not once, but several times. Tears are a language. My tears were expressing the grief I felt as I reflected on the nature of the tree of *my* life; grief that, throughout those years it had yielded such a bumper harvest of rotten fruit: blaming, accusing, criticising, judging to mention a few. As I wept, the knees of my heart bent at the foot of Christ's cross and I found myself praying the prayer, not of the Pharisee, but of the publican: 'God, have mercy on me, a sinner . . .' (Luke 18:13), 'Lord, have mercy on me *the* sinner.'

Sadly, bumper harvests of sour fruit are not rare. They are common even though Paul stresses the seriousness of the situation and warns: 'Let me tell you again as I have before, that anyone living that sort of life will not inherit the kingdom of God' (Gal 5:21, LB).

Hatred

'That sort of life', as Paul defines it, includes hatred and fighting, jealousy and anger. Or, more accurately, it means a misappropriation of hatred, anger, jealousy and other similar emotions for we need to be clear in our minds that these emotions are not wrong in themselves. Nurtured appropriately, they could all ripen into love. Take hatred, for example. When someone we love is hurt by the unkind or thoughtless words of another, hatred might burn in our bones – hatred, not of the person who caused the injury but hatred of the unkindness and the thoughtlessness that is wreaking such havoc. *This* hatred is not only appropriate, it is Christlike, curiously healing and tastes like sweet fruit. Channelled *destructively*, hatred is not simply sour, it poisons people's lives.

Think, for example, of the quarrel in the mountains that my husband and I had and that I described in chapter 3. In that chapter, I recalled how this caused my mood to swing from contentment to resentment. For a few hours after that quarrel, I was not only riddled with resentment but with hatred also. The incident reminded me that the dividing line between love and hate is gossamer thin. Indeed, hatred can displace love as fast as you can toss a coin. The reason for this is that hate is love hurting.

On that unforgettable day when we were enjoying the sun-splashed view to the full, revelling in God's creation and rejoicing in the companionship we so much enjoy when we give one another time, we had forgotten that love and hate are two sides of the same coin. Instead of nurturing affection by being attentive to one another and by being gentle with one another, we were both intent on pleasing ourselves. Consequently, without realising it, we unintentionally flicked the coin and watched it drop hate side up instead of love side up.

When love is hurt, the self-pitying, self-assertive, aggressive ego springs into action, rolls up its sleeves and fights. Anger rises like milk bubbling up in a pan. Impulsively, the hurt person channels their seemingly uncontrollable wrath in the direction of the offending person(s). Just as it is possible to prevent milk from boiling over by removing the pan from the hot ring, so it is possible to prevent hatred from spilling over – if we choose to. Think, for example, of what happens when the telephone rings while we are consumed with hatred for our spouse or a friend. We switch off the hatred and chat to the caller happily and helpfully. If we can do that when the phone rings, we can do it even when there are no interruptions – if we want to. On that beautiful day in the mountains, for example, just because David wanted one thing and I wanted another, I *need* not have sunk into a sulk. Even though I was hurting, I could have borne in mind Paul's ode to love: Love 'is not irritable or touchy. It does not hold grudges and will hardly even notice when others do it wrong' (1 Cor 13:5,7, LB). Instead of reacting, I could have paused, stared at the almond blossom and asked myself some adult questions: *What is going on here?*

Why am I hurting? What's the real problem? Whose problem is it? What am I really feeling? How can I convey those feelings to David in a way he can understand without being crushed? Had I done that, the surge of hatred would have been harmless. Indeed, far from becoming sour fruit, it would have ripened into the mature, refreshing fruit of love.

Jealousy

The picture that hangs like a back-cloth in my mind as I write is of a curious tree that grows near my home. 'Is it an orange tree or a lemon tree?' David and I have asked ourselves that question many, many times because, in season, both oranges *and* lemons hang from its branches simultaneously. When the fruit is young, it is impossible to tell which branches will bear lemons and which oranges. In their infancy and from a distance, both fruits look almost identical – both are small, leaf-green, hard, oval-round balls. It is as they grow and change colour that we discover which is which.

Just as the tree of our life can bear the sour fruit of hatred or the sweet fruit of love, so its fruit can ripen into trust or jealousy. We discover this when love is dented and we find ourselves kicking and screaming, squirming and fighting emotionally. We act in this violent way because hurt and fear spawn jealousy. One form of jealousy, as James reminds us, is wanting what we cannot have: 'You crave for something and don't get it; you are murderously jealous of what others have got and which you can't possess yourself; you struggle and fight one another' (James 4:2, JBP).

Today's newspapers, like yesterday's history books, are peppered with stories of individuals who glanced out of the corner of their eye and then took a long, leisurely look at another's wife or land or money or possessions or position or talents or opportunities in life and who wanted what they saw. They not only wanted what they saw, they found ways of acquiring what they wanted no matter by what means they achieved their goal. This facet of jealousy might stem from greed or it might stem from insecurity.

Insecurity often breeds lack of trust and lack of trust, in turn, can give rise to another form of jealousy that often paralyses close relationships: marriage and close friendships in particular. When consumed by this form of jealousy, a husband or a wife, a friend or a lover observes the loved one relating to another. The relationship might be totally innocent but fear and insecurity give rise to the suspicion that the observer's place in the loved one's affections and life are about to be or have actually been supplanted. Such suspicion engenders bitterness and gives birth to almost uncontrollable rage. And, as the writer of Proverbs shrewdly observes: 'Anger is cruel and fury overwhelming, but who can stand before jealousy?' (Prov 27:4).

David Mace uses the helpful phrase a 'protective emotion' to present the positive face of jealousy. Other protective emotions are fear – the emotion that persuades us to be careful when we cross a busy road – and the kind of nervousness that ensures that we prepare carefully before preaching a sermon or performing in public. Protective emotions have a negative face, though, as well as a positive one. They can induce so much fear that we panic and can't bring ourselves to cross that busy road. Or they can make us so nervous that stage fright tor-pedoes us – preventing us from preaching or performing in public. Or they can fill us with a jealousy that is so all-consuming that panic and rage can sweep over us with demonic strength. The panic and the rage set us fighting and kicking and screaming. Although our loved one protests pointing out that our fears are groundless or that we are being irrational, still we rant and rave in a frantic effort to fight off the impending doom of rejection. Alternatively, we feel so crushed by the slightest suspicion that we might be rejected that we withdraw or collapse in an emotional heap like a limp, deflated hot-air balloon. We fail to see what in our more rational moments we understand all too well that: 'a jealous wife [or friend or lover] is not an easy or pleasant person to live with. It is miserable to be constantly under suspicion – especially without cause. You don't feel warm and tender toward someone who is constantly spilling out resentment toward you and making false accusations against you. You feel thwarted, indignant, misunderstood.'[1]

Yet another form of jealousy fosters cut-throat competitiveness. Many marriages have been becalmed because the husband and wife compete with one another rather than seeking ways of complementing one another so one feels threatened or diminished when the other is praised or promoted in some way. Many Christian businesses flounder because, instead of finding God's plan for the firm and working that plan, they look over their shoulders at other similar companies, covet the financial rewards they enjoy and, in order to achieve similar success, compete even though this might mean straying from their God-given vision. And many missionary enterprises are thwarted because mission partners compete with one another rather than working alongside one another. Some become so possessive of the ministry they have pioneered that they not only refuse to include others in it, they actively strive to elbow others out.

Generation differences

Recent research by sociologists opens our eyes to the reasons why generation differences so easily give birth to possessiveness and divisiveness, jealousy and hatred, complaints and criticisms. The research divides society into four categories: Seniors, that is, those born before 1927, Boosters or Builders, that is, those born between 1927–1945, Boomers or Baby Boomers, those born between 1946–1964 in America or between 1951–1969 in Europe and Busters, or Generation X, today's generation.

If we reflect on the era in which Boosters were born, two world wars and their aftermath, years of recession, rationing, bereavement and improvisation, it will not surprise us to learn that Boosters grew up with a 'life will be hard' mentality that dogs them for the rest of their life; an attitude they carry into the whole of life. Because times were hard for them as they grew up, they expected to work hard to survive. Their attitude to life was a, 'he who works hard, eats' background. Creature comforts the majority of people in the West now take for granted – like a bathroom and hot running water or like a washing machine or a car were, for countless Boosters, luxuries that were enviable but not attainable. Leisure time, similarly, was a serendipity – at best strictly limited, at worst, non-existent. Business, of necessity, came before pleasure almost all of the time.

Baby Boomers, by contrast, were welcomed into a world that believed it had turned a corner. The war was over. The future looked promising – full of peace, plenty and prosperity. 'Life will be good' was the optimistic belief that filled the air they breathed. Born into comparative material affluence, Baby Boomers were beguiled into believing that consumer goods that had seemed like luxuries to their forebears were, in fact, their birthright; that ever-increasing leisure time with the financial resources that ensured that they could 'eat, drink and be merry' were also rights to be demanded. Motivated by the 'work hard and get rich' mentality, they looked for jobs that offered attractive financial benefits rather than work that was necessarily meaningful. Whereas mothers had once expected to stay at home to look after their children, the feminist outcry now encouraged countless women to pursue their own careers.

By the time the Buster generation bounced its way into the world, the scene had changed yet again. Busters have been described as 'the most indulged in material possessions and the most deprived of love and family support of all the generations. They are products of fragmented families, of families lacking time for real nurturing. They have often been victims of sexual abuse and other forms of violence.'[2] Let one of them speak for himself and his own generation:

> We are the ones who were not aborted or contracepted out of existence. We are the ones who . . . arrived just as the world was 'going bust' . . . We blame the generations of our parents and grandparents . . . for leaving us a social, economic and environmental mess to fix . . . We've grown up in an age of social malaise, urban decline, inept government, corrupt government, ineffective school systems, soaring national debt, increasing environmental concern, racial polarisation, high divorce rates and declining values . . . We have little respect for authority, whether at school, at church, on the job, in government or at home. But there is a big difference between us and our parents: whereas the Boomers of the sixties protected and attacked the system . . . my generation prefers to ignore or ridicule the system . . . For Generation X, the past is for ever beyond reach, the present is black and bleak, and the future is a brick wall.[3]

So writes Kevin Ford (son of evangelist Leighton Ford, nephew of Billy Graham, himself a Christian ministry consultant working among students) in his challenging, disturbing, powerful book *Jesus for a New Generation*. Quoting one of 'his' students, he adds: 'I don't think there is a future. There aren't any good jobs left. No good houses left. The planet's turning into a sewer. The rain forests are disappearing, the cities are falling apart, nuclear weapons are spreading through the Third World . . .'[4]

In other words, whereas Boosters believed that life would be hard and Boomers believed that life would be good, Busters believe that life will be so bad that you must salvage all you can from its ruins as quickly as possible. This attitude sours their approach to almost everything. You work because it is personally fulfilling and in order to earn life's biggest plus – time off. Work must never interfere with pleasure. And since finances will not be forthcoming to buy luxuries, you condemn them. In fact, you pooh-pooh anything that is unattainable.

Boosters, Boomers and Busters

Boosters, Boomers and Busters exist and attempt to co-exist in every strata of society. They seek to create Christian communities and church teams, fellowships and music groups, house groups and businesses and, of course, families.

I think, for example, of the delightful, scatty, fun-loving, twenty-year-old Buster who confided in me that her (Booster) grandmother's presence in the home was souring family relationships:

'Life at home's become unbearable since my gran moved in. She fusses over me as though I'm a little girl. She thinks I should be in by ten every night. She can't bear it if even faint strains of my radio reach her ears but she turns her television up full volume. And she's so demanding of my time; always expecting me to sit in her room and talk to her.'

'She expects me to be in by ten every night'. When Boosters were emerging from their teens, ten o'clock was late. For Busters, though, at ten o'clock, the evening has only just begun!

Or I think of another family I met within minutes of

writing the above. The father owns a restaurant in an idyllic part of Cyprus. Perched on the edge of a promontory, it affords a panoramic view of a fairy-tale mountain village. Sitting on the terrace on a tranquil, balmy, moon-lit evening is one of the delights of life on the island – for Boosters and Boomers. While waiting for a wedding anniversary meal to be served, however, the peace of the place was suddenly shattered by the thud of heavy rock music booming round the valley. 'Where's that noise coming from?' we complained to the owner. He shrugged his shoulders and smiled a wry smile. 'It's my nephew', he apologised. 'He's wanting to open a club for young people down below . . .' As the amicable conversation progressed, the Booster–Buster divide became more and more apparent. How long, I wondered, can the owner's dream of a peaceful, classy restaurant co-exist with his nephew's vision of a trendy place where Busters can come and dance away the fun-filled night? Who will have to give way to whom?

The Booster, Boomer, Buster divide affects office politics too. Kevin Ford helpfully catapults us, in our imagination, into the office of a Christian managing director, Tom Hooper:

Tom Hooper sat in his oak-panelled office behind his big oak desk, a huge stylised painting of the Gutenberg printing press at his back. 'Peter,' he said with a troubled expression, 'you know I've tried to run this business as a Christian business. I try to honour God by the excellence of our service and by the way I treat my employees.'

'Absolutely,' Peter agreed, sitting in one of the plush upholstered chairs opposite the desk . . .

The conversation is interrupted by Kevin, a young mid-to-late twenties employee. Tom Hooper goes on to share with both Peter and Kevin a personnel crisis that has been brewing for months.

'I've interviewed a dozen people, and I wouldn't employ any of them. Fact is, I felt as if they were interviewing me! Do you know the kinds of questions they asked me? "Will I be valued as a person?" And "How much holiday do I get?" Five of 'em told me, "I've got to have my weekends free." I mean, whatever happened to drive and ambition and wanting to get ahead?'

Peter shrugged. 'Maybe young adults today aren't as career obsessed as you and me?'

'Peter's right,' said Kevin. 'Most of my friends are more into personal fulfilment than money . . .'

'Why is that?' asked Hooper. They discuss an employee, Michael, who has just left the firm. 'I mean, why are people like Michael the way they are? The man is competent enough at his job, but he wants to put in his forty hours a week and that's it. No extra initiative, no drive, no ambition. I don't think he's lazy, exactly.'

'No,' said Kevin. 'Michael's not lazy. He did his job and did it well.'

'But he has no respect for authority,' Tom Hooper growled . . .

'Maybe it's an age thing,' said Peter. 'A generation thing. I'm used to thinking of "Baby Boomer" as the equivalent of youth and young thinking. But lately whenever I talk to my college-age son, Ben, I start feeling pretty old and creaky. Ben and his whole generation seem to have a different outlook than I do – different than I had when I was his age.'

'Maybe you're right,' said Hooper. 'Maybe it is a generational thing. These – what do you call 'em? Baby Busters, isn't it? – we've got a lot of 'em working around here. And if there's one thing I've observed about them as a class – present company excepted, Kevin – is that so many of them seem to be cynical, unmotivated and self-centred. They don't seem to care about money or promotion. They complain about how hard it is to find a good job. Then they leave a good job rather than getting a haircut or giving up wearing a silly looking nose ring. Trying to figure out this generation is like trying to nail jelly to a wall! . . . What do these people want?' . . .

'What they want is quite simple,' said Kevin. 'They want to do their job, take home their money and have a life. They don't want their job to be their life. They want life to be their life. I hear it all the time from their friends . . . I believe there are ways to motivate them – if you just take time to understand them.'

'Oh?' Tom Hooper was interested.

'This is the MTV generation with a short attention span – so why not find ways to give them shorter, more stimulating projects . . . Why not give them feedback every so often – you know, like a video game score? Let them know once in a while that they're doing a good job. List the names of the top employees each month, together with their performance ratings . . . And [because] they feel shut out of the system . . . why not give them ongoing leadership training and a sense that maybe their jobs can lead somewhere after all? They think no one cares about their families, so why not offer them good, well-supervised-on-site child care? . . . The people in my generation like fun . . . How about making this place more fun to work in? I mean, everything doesn't have to be so starchy and serious. Let's put up some corkboards around the office and pin up some cartoons. Let's have employee birthday parties. Some unexpected rewards for a job well done. A company picnic at the lake with some football or volleyball.'

'Those are great ideas,' added Peter.

'I don't know,' said Hooper. ' I just don't know.'[5]

Just as Booster Tom Hooper's conversation with his

younger colleagues left him puzzled, so many Booster leaders of missionary organisations find themselves bemused by Boomer and Buster members of their organisations. Bearing in mind the background I have sketched, the reason is not hard to unearth. The Booster generation gave birth to 'the traditional missionary': Christians who were single-minded, task-oriented, 'prepared to put career and family on the altar for the sake of the gospel.'[6] Like the pioneers they were, they planted churches, started schools, trained pastors and endured great hardship in previously unevangelised parts of the world. They laid a magnificent foundation on which today's Christians now build. But the price they paid is incalculable. They seemed to sacrifice any-one and anything 'for the kingdom': personal prefer-ences, creature comforts, family time, friendships, per-sonal prayer and resourcing, to mention a few. 'Saved to serve', 'don't let your marriage interfere with your ministry' – these were the slogans that goaded them to go on and on giving until they dropped.

Leaders of many of today's missionary organisa-tions are Boosters whose lives are also governed by this mind-set. When new missionaries question and chal-lenge policies rather than meekly submitting and co-operating as their predecessors would have done, Booster leaders frequently find themselves floundering and determining to make the younger generation 'see sense'. They rarely realise that such attempts are futile because Baby Boomers have been conditioned to take as their motto, 'I have a duty to myself': a mind-set that seems programmed to clash with their forebears. Far from being prepared to sacrifice their job or their fami-lies for the sake of the gospel, they place a heavy emphasis on using their God-given skills to the full. If someone denies them the opportunity of using their expertise, they act like caged animals – either resorting to aggression or, conversely, becoming depressed. If they have children, unlike their forebears, many flatly refuse to send them to boarding schools. Believing that parents are the ones to care for their children, their abhorrence for absentee mothers and fathers runs deep and prompts them to wax eloquent on the subject. So much so that many expect to donate a considerable amount of time to educating their offspring at home.

Boomers are different from their Booster forebears in other ways, too. Unlike Boosters, they are not rugged individualists, they expect to play a significant team role. Boosters followed their leader simply because he was the leader ('After all,' I have heard Boosters say, 'he is the one with the information'), but because information is as much at their finger-tips as those of their leaders, Boomers, question and challenge and confront in a way that leaves many Boosters scandalised. To add insult to injury, Boomers characteristically want to find out how it feels to become a mission partner before they actually commit themselves to becoming one. Short-term experience programmes are therefore 'in' – long-term service a no-go area. 'But whatever happened to *commitment*?' Boosters protest. While they still search for an answer to this question Busters spring centre stage presenting Boosters and Boomers alike with a fresh set of challenges and, for some, headaches, at best, and, at worst, unresolved and seemingly unresolvable friction.

> Out of [the Buster] generation come missionary applicants from broken homes who often have a great deal of pain . . . to work through and who may be particularly vulnerable to emotional problems on the field. They may come across as self-centred, being unwilling to be over-loaded in their work and being very sensitive to any perception of rejection. They may insist on living 'balanced' lives even in situations where this can only be done at others' expense. However, this flows not from selfishness but from a fear that they will not cope if overloaded.[7]

Busters also come with expectations that can raise the hackles of both Boosters and Boomers. In expecting and needing to be part of a team, they also expect to have access to information that would formerly have been considered confidential, they expect to be given the opportunity of challenging rather than automatically accepting the policies they gain access to *and* they expect their leaders to lack integrity – expectations and assumptions that disturb many Boosters so deeply that they are left reeling with shock. Their claims can sound so self-opinionated and cut-and-dried that Boosters recoil further. Take this claim for example:

> To my generation, the problems of the world are too complex for us to solve. In response we shun global strategies, ambitious goals and great causes . . . Those of us who are inclined towards do-goodism will perform do-gooder acts on a smaller, simpler scale: instead of trying to eliminate homelessness through the nation, we will feed one homeless person in the park. That is an active solution, a tangible solution, a simple solution.[8]

Busters also ruffle more than a few team feathers by insisting on introducing fun into team activities. For those brought up in the 'business before pleasure' era, this insistence on fun-filled activities is anathema – yet another source of conflict.

Yet, as one Booster missionary insists, we need Generation X, 'if we lose them, we are losing some of our potentially most creative and effective missionaries'.[9]

Cross-cultural differences

Just as you don't have to be working overseas to be faced with the challenge of wrestling with cross-generation differences, neither do you have to be working overseas to be confronted with cross-cultural differences. Many teams in many countries these days are made up of individuals from a whole variety of races and cultures. The potential is enriching – the practicalities often perplexing and problematic. The team will almost certainly bump into language barriers for one thing. English-speaking people from a variety of countries might be thrown into confusion, for example, because different countries use the same word or phrase differently. I think, for instance, of the word 'lay-by' that I used in the title of one of my books: *Finding God in the Fast Lane as well as in life's lay-bys*.[10] A lay-by for people in England means a place within yards of a main road onto which motorists can drive and park their car when they need a rest. In New Zealand, I discovered *after* the book had been published, 'lay-by' means something entirely different. If someone wants to reserve rather than buy outright, say, some balls of wool or an item of clothing, they ask the shop assistant to put the article(s) in a lay-by for them! And which of us have not been amused when the English talk about putting their luggage in the *boot* of their car while their American counterparts talk about putting their luggage in the *trunk*? Or what English person has not smiled when they hear the American word 'sack lunch' meaning 'a picnic'?

Another language hazard is that people whose first language is not English may cause offence as a result. Marjory Foyle, a psychiatrist with years of experience working overseas remembers how 'a Scandinavian nurse once told me that a ward into which I had put a great deal of effort was "revolting". I began to bristle – until God reminded me to ask her what she meant. I discovered she was only trying to say it was a bit dilapidated and needed white-washing!'[11]

Language differences pose another problem. They inevitably necessitate one person or another discussing, negotiating, learning, even praying aloud in a language that is not their mother-tongue. Only those who have had to do it know how exhausting and limiting this can be. In fact, it is now widely accepted that communicating across language and culture barriers is one of the major contributing stress factors that plague all who work in cross-cultural environments, especially mission partners.[12]

Then, of course, people from different cultures will bring to the team a different set of norms. With disarming honesty, Marjory Foyle again paints the picture so well:

> I once worked in a hospital whose staff came from nine different countries. One Good Friday, I was horrified to discover that all the men on the hospital building site had come to work. The missionary in charge, in working clothes, was busily getting them organized. I was incensed and became very critical, because in my own background, Good Friday had always been a very special day that Christians spent in a long church service, or in prayer or meditation at home. I thought to myself, 'He can't be much of a Christian.' Later, God taught me that not only was he a much better person than I, but that in his country Good Friday was not observed in this way.[13]

We smile or nod our head wisely when we hear and recall such stories. Being caught in the crossfire of culturally sensitive clashes, however, is far from funny at the time. On the contrary, it can feel excruciatingly painful. It is all too easy to hit deadlock. I was reminded of this when I heard a young man sigh: '*Here we go again!*' when he and his colleague from a different culture were attempting, unsuccessfully, to plan an important cross-cultural social event. The words sounded innocent enough but, as he spoke his body betrayed the depth of his feelings. His face flushed with anger, he clenched his fists as though he wanted to thump them on the table or hit someone with them and his eyes were full of pained desperation.

Yes. Working in a cross-cultural team can be as exasperating as it is enriching. Add to the cross-cultural challenge, the cross-generation challenge and you have such a vast range of questions being asked and assumptions being made that it is little wonder that some individualists want one thing – OUT! Yet Paul prays: 'May the God of steadfastness and encouragement grant you to live in such harmony with one another . . . that together you may with one voice glorify the God and Father of our Lord Jesus Christ. Welcome one another, therefore, as Christ has welcomed you, for the glory of God' (Rom 15:5–7, RSV).

He also reminds us that 'each of us is a part of the one body of Christ. Some of us are Jews and some are Gentiles, some are slaves and some are free. But the Holy Spirit has fitted us all together into one body. We have been baptized into Christ's body by the one Spirit, and have all been given that same Holy Spirit (1 Cor 12:12–13, LB).

Mission teams, whether at home or overseas, face yet another challenge. Different mission members come from different church backgrounds, each with their own particular emphasis. So some such mission teams threaten to fracture because of theology or perceptions of the way God works. Some members of a group, for example, might insist that new believers must be publicly baptised while other members of the same group might equally insist that such a public declaration of faith is not culturally sensitive. Or some members of the group might insist that converts should be encouraged to pray in tongues whereas other members of the same team might throw up their hands in horror at the mere mention of subjects like 'baptism in the Spirit'.

Because mission teams exist to bring people into God's kingdom the fiercest battles of all are fought over these theological issues. Watching such battles from the sidelines can be particularly heart-breaking. Watching Christians tearing one another apart is never easy; sinking one's teeth into the sour fruit of blaming and attacking, detachment and gossip is never pleasant.

Blaming and gossip

When contests of this nature erupt, our instinctive reaction is to find someone to blame: a scapegoat to accuse: 'Its all your fault'. In other words, we recognise the problem but we refuse to acknowledge that we have contributed to that problem in any way. When we take this view, others become the villains and our own thoughts and behaviour are exonerated. The more we fail to accept responsibility for our own culpability, the more we magnify the part played by others. As Scott-Peck puts it in *People of the Lie*: 'Since [we] must deny [our] own badness, [we] must perceive others as bad.'[14] Blaming leads to attacking as naturally as melting snow creates an avalanche. And when someone is attacked they recoil, freeze, withdraw – unable to cope with the welter of their own emotions.

Seeking to place a distance between ourselves and someone with whom we are at variance is sometimes called defensive detachment. Defensive detachment results, often, in devious behaviour.

When there is a gulf between you and another person, instead of sitting next to that person in church as you might have done in the past, you sit on the opposite side of the building if at all possible. Or, if you see them coming down the road while you are in town, you cross over to the other side of the street as quickly as you can. If he or she is speaking at a conference you are attending, you might even boycott the meetings that person is addressing, criticise him or her behind their back and generally creating havoc with that mis-

chievous little part of your body, the tongue. You conveniently forget Jesus' injunction:

> 'Don't pick on people, jump on their failures, criti-
> cise their faults – unless, of course, you want the
> same treatment. That critical spirit has a way of
> boomeranging. It's easy to see a smudge on your
> neighbour's face and be oblivious to the ugly sneer
> on your own. Do you have the nerve to say, "Let me
> wash your face for you," when your own face is dis-
> torted with contempt? . . . Wipe that ugly sneer off
> your own face, and you might be fit to offer a wash-
> cloth to your neighbour.'
>
> (Matt 7:1, *The Message*)

Sadly, most of us are slow to wipe the sneer off our
own faces. We fall, instead, into the trap of gossip.
Think back to chapter 4, for example, where I described
the division that grew between Pastor Jeremy and his
assistant Paul. The more Paul and Anne felt the sting of
the seeming rejection I described, the more they talked
about the disintegrating relationship with Jeremy and
his wife. Unfortunately, they talked, not just to one
another, they gossiped to members of the church as
well. The result was inevitable. People adopted a
piggy-in-the-middle mentality. Factions formed: the
pro-Paul's and the pro-Jeremy's. Such splinter groups
need not have divided the congregation if Paul and
Anne had acted on Jesus' clear instructions: 'If you are
offering your gift at the altar and there remember that
your brother [or sister] has something against you,
leave your gift there in front of the altar. First go and be
reconciled to your brother [or sister]; then come and
offer your gift' (Matt 5:23). 'If a fellow believer hurts
you, *go and tell him [or her]* – work it out between the
two of you' (Matt 18:15, *The Message*, emphasis mine).

'Go and tell him [or her]' – that's the key. Instead of
telling Jeremy and his wife how they felt, Paul and

Anne did what most of us do in similar circumstances: they told one another how they felt colluding with one another in the process and they talked to many others in the church. In doing so, as so often happens in such circumstances, the conflict escalated.

Distancing, divergence and destruction

David Cormack helps us to understand how such divisions deepen. The following diagram illustrates his thesis:

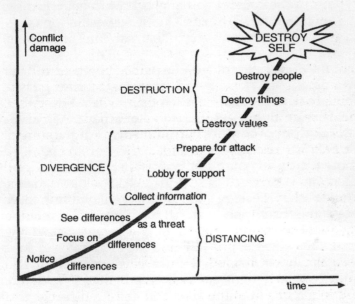

Conflict-Escalation Curve or Blast-off![15]

Two or more people who clash or who grate on one another become increasingly hostile towards one another and consequently become increasingly conscious of the differences that divide them: cultural differences, religious differences, personality differences, generation differences, language barriers and so on.

They become curiously blind to any goodness in the person or people with whom they are at variance. Unless their differences are dealt with, they home in on these differences, concentrate on them, perceive them as a threat and begin to build up a case against the 'enemy' by collecting information about them. The inevitable result of this witch-hunt is that the parties concerned distance themselves from one another. The distancing phase may last for minutes, hours, days, months or even years depending on the nature of the disharmony. The door to communication closes firmly. The course the conflict will take is now determined by feelings rather than by facts. Unless reconciliation takes place, the conflict will inevitably escalate and move into the divergence phase.

In the divergence phase, the parties involved roll up their emotional sleeves and prepare to attack. They lobby for support to strengthen their own position and openly refer to the person with whom they are in collision as an opponent, even an enemy. Any common ground that used to (and still could) unite them, is ignored. Instead, they not only enlist the support of others, they strive to ensure that their 'side' remains loyal to the cause of undermining, devaluing and destroying their opponents. The conflict is now becoming public property instead of the private, personal affair it once was.

Again, unless someone intervenes and reconciliation takes place, all parties concerned move steadily up the strife curve and into the third and final phase, the destructive phase: the destruction, not only of people and possessions, but of values also. As David Cormack puts it: 'Eventually parties . . . use all the weapons at their disposal . . . Families and one-time friends tear their relationship and themselves apart in pursuit of victory.' In this fiercest and final stage of unresolved conflict, the parties lose all their reference points: Christians act like demons; freedom fighters act like oppressors; and those who fight for peace learn only the skills of war. Mutual destruction is the end of all-out conflict . . . Whether between nations or within churches or families, phase three conflict is mutually destructive. It serves no good purpose. Even if it is seen as a way of resolving the continuing exchanges between two strong, opposing parties, phase three conflict cannot easily be contained. There is a saying in Swahili that where two elephants fight, the grass gets hurt. To engage in self-destruction is evil, and it is worse to commit innocent parties to the same fate.[16]

And yet, again and again we witness the destruction phase being played out before our very eyes: in our churches, in our fellowship groups, among friends, in our ministry teams at home and overseas. Is it any wonder that, as Christians, we find ourselves enraged, full of anger?

Our next task is to take a long, careful look at anger. Before that, however, this might be an appropriate time to pause and to take a careful look at your own life – particularly at any unresolved conflicts that might have prompted you to pick up this book in the first place.

Suggested exercises

1. Think, for example, of the various emotions we have placed under the microscope in this chapter. The first was hatred. Think back to occasions when hatred rose up from the depths of your heart and ask yourself the following questions:
• Why was I hurting?
• What was the nub of the problem?
• Whose problem was it, mine or ....?
• What were the feelings that gave birth to the

hatred?
• How might I have conveyed those feelings to the person(s) concerned without crushing them? How could I have helped them understand me?

2. Or think of the section on jealousy. Re-read it.

• Ask God to show you whether you are falling into the trap of wanting material possessions or relationships or positions of leadership or power or prestige so much that you are falling into the trap James describes in chapter 4:2 of his letter.
• Or if the jealousy that doubts the integrity of a loved one eats at your heart, look back at chapter 2 – the chapter on inner conflict. Write down your fears. Face them. Spread them before God. If necessary, talk them through with a friend or counsellor who can help you grow through the crisis.
• Ask yourself whether unhealed hurts from the past or a low self-image have given rise to this distressing emotion. Look back at the Dynamic Cycle of Being and Well-Being (p 41). Ask God for the grace to take the pain to him so that he can console you with his accepting, sustaining love. Or resolve to share the hurt with someone skilled enough to help you grow through it.

3. Reflect on the Boosters, Boomers and Busters section. Can you think of occasions when you have witnessed generation clashes like the ones I have quoted? How did you feel about them? How do you think the people involved could have grown in their understanding of each other? Where do *you* need to grow in your understanding of others – particularly those from a different generation or culture?

4. Re-read, then reflect on the final part of the chapter. Think carefully about the three major phases in

the development of unresolved conflict. Then look carefully at the Strife Curve before asking yourself:

- Are any of my relationships at the distancing stage – focusing on the differences that divide rather than the factors that could provide a foundation for unity?
- In my family, my friendships, the church, the neighbourhood, are any of my relationships moving up the strife curve into the divergence phase? If so, am I rolling up my emotional sleeves and strengthening my position? If so, why? What am I aiming to achieve?
- Have any of my relationships so hurtled out of control that I'm in the destruction phase – intent on punishing, even destroying 'the enemy'?
- What do I propose to do with my findings?
- Take a look at the following diagram commonly known as The Johari Window. Consider its implications. Do they influence in any way how you might process the findings that have come to light for you as you have been reading this book and doing the exercises?

		OPEN	**BLIND**
How I might start a relation- ship	known to my friend	Things I see about myself which I share with the other	Things I cannot see about myself but which the other sees
	not known to my friend	**SECRET** Things I see about myself but which I keep from the other	**UNKNOWN** Things which neither I nor the other know about myself

THE JOHARI WINDOW
Growth Through Dialogue

The genius of the Johari Window is that it invites us to look through an imaginary window that has four panes in it. The public pane refers to those parts of myself that are known to me and that are equally obvious to others – like, whether I am an extravert or an introvert, whether I take an interest in the way I dress or whether I just throw on whatever garment happens to be lying around in the morning. The blind or hidden pane, conversely, refers to parts of myself that I am unaware of: blindspots that prevent me from detecting mannerisms that are glaringly obvious to others but that remain hidden from me – like that irritating habit I may have of drumming my fingers on the table when someone is talking to me or of humming loudly when everyone else in the group is seeking stillness.

The private pane indicates that part of me that I normally hide – my secret self that conceals my fears and failures, dreams and despairs, hurts and sensitivities, childlike delights and revelations from God – and my deepest, innermost feelings. In other words, the private pane opens onto that part of me that is uniquely 'mine' and that I may prefer to share with no one. Instead, I will don a mask when I am not at home in this room so that no one will be able even to guess what I am really like. If I am a sensitive nurse who cares deeply when a patient suffers or when one dies, for example, I may cover my caring self with a camouflage of cold efficiency rather than reveal the ache in my heart.

Finally, the unknown pane indicates another area that remains a mystery to myself and others. The psalmist calls this 'the inmost place' (Ps 51:6) or 'the heart' (Ps 139:23). Paul labels it the 'old self' (Eph 4:22) or 'the earthly nature' (Col 3:5). Childhood hurts, like wounded children, often lie suffering in this subconscious place. So do attitudes and inclinations that baffle

126

me and that I cannot access without the aid of the ministry of the Holy Spirit who may choose to reveal its contents to me directly or through dialogue with a friend, a spouse, a counsellor, a psychotherapist, a psychologist, a growth group, to mention a few possibilities. When such dialogue takes place, it might encourage me to draw the curtains of the private and the blind parts of my life. I might open those curtains ever so slightly, just wide enough to understand myself better and to pave the way for a spurt of growth:

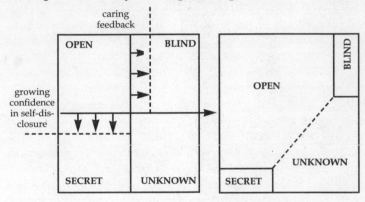

The result of open-sharing and feedback

5. As a result of reading this chapter, instead of just looking at the four window panes, open them, as it were, by writing in them. First scribble in the 'public pane' those facts about yourself that are patently obvious to you and to others: the colour of your eyes and hair, for example; your height, your most obvious likes and dislikes. Next, if you can pluck up the courage, sit down with a sensitive friend or a member of your family and ask them to name one or two things that you could write in the 'blind pane'. Restrict the number to two in the first instance because such revelations can be unexpectedly

painful. Little by little you can add more.

In a quiet moment, write in the 'private pane', in invisible ink if need be, words that sum up your secret self and finally, ask the Holy Spirit to show you as much of your unknown self as God wants you to see at this moment in time.

The result of this exercise could be, not only that you grow in self-awareness but that you also experience the kind of openness that leads to a growth in intimacy.

6

ANOTHER FRUIT:
ANGER

Perhaps anger should have been included in the last chapter? After all, anger is similar to hatred and jealousy in that, it, too, of itself, is a natural, neutral, involuntary reaction to an event, a conversation or set of circumstances. Like hatred and jealousy, anger can trigger wild, uncontrolled behaviour that is as terrifying as an electric storm. Its thunder claps rumble round our mind, its lightning terrifies our soul, its gale-force wind howls through our senses, its hail-stones lash our bodies, leaving us helpless. Yet, just as an electric thunderstorm is often precisely what is needed to clear the air of humidity and oppressive heat, so anger is often necessary to clear our minds, to purge our hearts and to calm our fears. In other words, to return to the metaphor we used in the last chapter, anger can ripen into a sweet fruit or it can become a sour one. Everything depends on what we do with it.

Processing anger is not unlike attending to fruit. I think, for example of the vine outside my garden gate. As I write, its buds are bursting into leaf – virgin green leaves that shimmer in the warm sunshine and slender green flowers, the size of my little finger – the harbingers of would-be grapes. Although the vine throbs with potential, unless someone prunes, sprays and feeds it, in four months time, when the harvest is being gathered, it will be over-laden with unsupported, leggy branches that will sap its energy. Such fruit that ripens will taste bitter or will shrivel before it has

...ime to mature. Wizened, diseased grapes will angle from those branches like bunches of dried-up sultanas. Just as the vine needs the skills of an experienced vine-dresser, so emotions need the skills of those who can handle them with care. Perhaps this applies more to anger than to any other emotion. Before we can discover how to deal with this powerful emotion, however, we need to establish precisely what anger is.

Anger is . . .

Ask many Christians the question, 'What is anger?' and their knee-jerk response will be, 'It's a sin'. As we have already seen, though, and as David Augsburger argues in *Anger and Assertiveness in Pastoral Care*, 'there are no good or bad feelings; feelings simply *are*'[1] – just like the farmer's grapes.

Whether a feeling becomes good or bad, whether it becomes sweet or sour fruit depends on how it is expressed. As Augsburger persists:

> The central issue, then, is not *whether* one experiences negative emotions, but *how*; not *if* one dare become angry, but in what *way*. To be fully aware of one's anger or hate, and to be free to integrate it in ways that are both powerful and respectful, is to be vitally alive. To be truly alert to effective ways of channelling these emotions creatively is to be authentically present with others and prizing of the self.[2]

Or, as Richard Walters reminds us, anger is often a reflex action. It rises to the surface so swiftly that we have no conscious control over its arrival so 'we should not feel guilty about this'.[3] Claims like these may startle readers who have been brought up in the 'anger is a sin' school. Look at it this way. If anger, of itself, was a sin, would Jesus have burned with resentment? Or would Paul have written: '*In your anger* do not sin' (Eph 4:26, emphasis mine)? Surely not? Paul clearly *expects* us to be angry. He also challenges us to find ways of processing and channelling our anger – ways that are constructive and not destructive; ways that keep us from sinning, that is, ways that keep us from disobeying God, crushing others or manipulating situations so that the world revolves around ourselves rather than around God; ways that ensure that anger accelerates the growth in us of the fruit of the Spirit: love, joy, peace, patience, kindness and self-control (Gal 5:22).

Biblical definitions

'If anger isn't a sin, what is it?' That's a question puzzled people often ask. We find our first clue in the New Testament. As Richard Walters helpfully reminds us, the two most frequently used words for anger in the New Testament are *thymos* and *orge*. *Thymos* is used some twenty times and conveys a mixture of meanings: turbulent commotion, boiling agitation, a sudden emotional explosion or eruption, the opposite of peace. The English word that most accurately sums up *thymos* is rage, for rage is that violent, over-heated, outward expression of anger that manifests itself in violent outbursts.

The writer to the Hebrews uses the word *thymos* when praising the faith of Moses: 'By an act of faith, he turned his heel on Egypt, indifferent to the king's blind rage' (Heb 11:27, *The Message*).

Paul also uses *thymos* in 2 Corinthians 12:20 when writing to the Christians in Corinth: 'I do admit that I have fears that when I come you'll disappoint me and I'll disappoint you, and in frustration with each other everything will fall to pieces – quarrels, jealousy, flaring tempers, taking sides, angry words, vicious rumors, swelled heads and general bedlam' (*The Message*).

131

While *thymos* refers to the outward expression of anger we call rage, *orge* means a long-lasting attitude that continues to seek revenge. *Orge* appears in the New Testament forty-five times. Its nearest parallel in the English language is resentment – that seething emotion that we attempt to suppress it, but that is rather like weeds lurking under a patio: it pops through the cracks and crevices of our behaviour with monotonous regularity as well as with rigour.

Jesus uses *orge* when he insists: 'You're familiar with the command to the ancients, "Do not murder." I'm telling you that anyone who is so much as angry with a brother or sister is guilty of murder' (Matt 5:22, *The Message*). He uses the word in Luke 15, too, when describing the reaction of the elder brother to the party his father threw in celebration of the prodigal's return. And it is *orge* that is used in Ephesians 4:26: 'Be angry but do not sin.'

The New Testament occasionally uses a third word when referring to anger: *aganaktesis*. Used just five times, this word corresponds to the English indignation, that energetic, righteous reaction to the evils, horrors and injustices with which our world is rampant; that expression of anger that motivated men like Dr Barnardo and William Wilberforce to stem the tide of homelessness by establishing orphanages for starving street kids; that costly determination to right the wrongs that have been done to those they cared about that inspired women like Florence Nightingale to transform the squalor and stench of the hospital in Scutari into a place of healing, and Diana, Princess of Wales, to campaign against the land-mines that have killed and maimed so may innocent children and adults this century.

Richard Walters sums up the three faces of anger in this memorable way: 'While rage and resentment are aggressive, seeking to destroy their target, indignation seeks to mobilise the forces of good to challenge and defeat the forces of destruction and oppression. Indignation is the opposite of complacent acceptance of evil conditions.'[4]

Indignation

Bottled-up indignation burst out of Jesus as he witnessed the injustice that had become part and parcel of life in the Temple precincts in Jerusalem. Picture the scene as John describes it. Jesus, the sinless One, wanders into the outer court of the Temple – the only place where Gentiles are allowed to worship. The court is teeming with people: pilgrims, money-changers and sellers of sheep, cattle and doves. So the Prince of Peace makes a whip out of strips of leather or cord, drives men and cattle, sheep and doves out of the Temple and overturns the 'tables of the loan sharks' (John 2:15, The Message), scattering coins right, left and centre in the process. 'Get these out of here!', he yells. 'How dare you turn my Father's house into a market!' (John 2:16). Jesus is not losing his temper here. He *is* blazing with indignation. Consequently, he channels his bottled-up energy into a creative restoration of the Temple to its rightful use (John 2:17), makes a bid to rescue the poor from being exploited and ushers in the Kingdom by making it possible for all nations to worship in his Father's designated House of Prayer. Such indignation is totally appropriate for indignation is the proper reaction to injustice when it energises us to do all in our power to bring about changes that will rescue others from being abused, trampled on and unnecessarily hurt.

Summing up the three facets of anger referred to so frequently in the New Testament, Richard Walters concludes:

Rage seeks to do wrong, resentment seeks to hide wrong, indignation seeks to correct wrongs.

Rage and resentment seek to destroy people, indignation seeks to destroy evil.

Rage and resentment seek vengeance, indignation seeks justice.

Rage is guided by selfishness, resentment is guided by cowardice, indignation is guided by mercy.

Rage uses open warfare, resentment is a guerilla fighter, indignation is an honest and fearless and forceful defender of truth.

Rage defends itself, resentment defends the status quo, indignation defends the other person.[5]

Among Christians, he observes, 'there is a fear of rage, a surplus of resentment and a shortage of indignation'[6] for the common pattern among Christians is to deny that they are angry, to suppress unacknowledged rage even though it continues to smoulder and turns to resentment that, in turn leads to tension and the determination, when the time is ripe, to seek revenge.

... a secondary emotion

Anger is not only energy, not simply an emotion, it is a *secondary* emotion. A secondary emotion implies the presence of a primary emotion – that is, the source emotion from which the anger flows. The implications of this are far-reaching. When someone is angry, we can either focus on the expressed rage or the seething resentment or the indignation or we can focus on the unexpressed primary emotion that triggered the energetic reaction in the first place. When tracing anger back to its source, we almost always discover rejection, fear or hurt. Jesus, for example, full of compassion for the marginalised as he was, doubtless felt deeply hurt because the poor were being fleeced in the Temple, of all places, and in the name of God. When we are dealing with anger, then, we need to learn the difficult art of unearthing the underlying cause. When the hurt is healed, the fear or injustice dealt with or the pain of rejection touched, the storm of anger will automatically blow itself out.

. . . an automatic response to danger

David and Vera Mace suggest yet another answer to the question: 'What is anger?' They claim in *Love and Anger in Marriage* that anger is an automatic response to perceived danger. In other words, you can't make yourself angry. Anger has to be triggered by something or someone. They go on to assert that we are never therefore responsible for being in a state of anger. We are only responsible for what we do with our anger after our conscious mind has taken over. They conclude from this what we have already noted, that 'it cannot be said that anger is sinful. Anger can be used to commit sin, to be sure, but that is an entirely different matter.'[7] Anger as they perceive it, is part of our in-built, in-grained survival kit – 'part of a complex system of resources that becomes available when we are in a state of stress.'[8] They remind us that the animal world resorts to a less sophisticated survival kit – like the sparrows in my garden, for example.

I watched their automatic response to danger one day while I was sitting in the place where I like to pray: a hushed, sun-kissed corner of the patio where the jasmine's scent rises from the pergola like incense. Suddenly, my peace was shattered by the frantic screeching of a gaggle of these agitated birds. Instinctively, my eyes turned to the birds' nest outside my study window. For weeks the parent birds had watched that nest jealously. Sure enough, these two, accompanied by countless others, were squawking and shouting, shrieking and swearing, their beaks all ajar, their bodies quivering and their small wings flapping furiously. Clearly they were terrified, stressed – and angry?

135

'Why the commotion?' I asked myself.

I looked this way and that but could discern no obvious cause for their concern. Sometime later, though, as I went out of my front door, I heard a curious plop behind me as something fell to the ground. Wheeling round, my heart froze. There on the ground beside me lay the long, black, coiled-up body of a snake. The sound and movement of the door must have frightened it as it lay sun-bathing on the flat roof of our home. Quick as lightning, it scaled the wall leading to the roof-top veranda. 'The flat roof,' I thought, when I had recovered from the shock. 'That's immediately above the birds' nest. Those birds must have seen the snake slither from the neighbour's garden onto the roof and, knowing that snakes love birds' eggs, set up a hullabaloo to protect their young from their predator.'

. . . a signal

Just as the world of nature has been endowed with the emotion of anger, so have new-born babies. How often we see their angelic faces pucker with pain and, if the pain is not relieved, turn scarlet with rage. As we watch the infant betray unmistakable signs of anger and as we watch its body writhe, we don't spank it for hurting, we attempt to relieve it of wind. Yet, when older children, teenagers or adults similarly manifest the anger born of pain, many of us criticise them: 'You shouldn't feel angry . . .' Or, if the anger is our own, we berate ourselves believing somehow that the emotion, of itself, is unacceptable.

If, however, anger is an automatic response to a signal that something is amiss, it follows that, in reproving ourselves and rebuking others in this way, we are acting somewhat unwisely – even foolishly. As Harriet Goldhor Lerner begins her book on anger:

Anger is a signal, and one worth listening to. Our anger may be a message that we are being hurt, that our rights are being violated, that our needs or wants are not being adequately met, or simply that something is not right. Our anger may tell us that we are not addressing an important emotional issue in our lives, or that too much of ourself – our beliefs, values, desires, or ambitions – is being compromised in a relationship. Our anger may be a signal that we are doing more and giving more than we can comfortably do or give. Or our anger may warn us that others are doing too much for us, at the expense of our own competence and growth. Just as physical pain tells us to take our hand off the hot stove, the pain of our anger preserves the very integrity of our self.[9]

Processing anger

If all these claims are true, it follows that many of us need to discover new ways of handling this electric emotion for Richard Walters is surely correct when he claims, 'It is okay to feel anger. It is not okay to keep on feeling it. We cannot avoid feeling angry, but we are commanded to deal with it properly.'[10] One vital way of 'dealing with it properly' is to recognise anger when it thrashes around in us; to have the integrity to acknowledge, at least to ourselves, 'I am *angry*'. Many people balk at making this admission. They prefer to deny anger's existence. 'I'm *never* angry,' they insist – usually, ironically, with considerable force that, in itself denotes repressed anger!

Such denial is hardly surprising in those who have come through the 'anger is a sin' school. It needs to be supplanted, though, not only with a recognition and admission of anger, 'I am angry', but with an *owning* of anger. '*I* am angry.' For many of us, this, too, will go against the grain. As we noted in an earlier chapter, almost all of us, when we clash with someone, look for someone other than ourselves on whom to pin the blame. We therefore play a subtle game of 'let's pretend'. 'Let's pretend that I'm angry because someone else or something else has *made* me angry.' We may not even realise that this is what we are doing. Nevertheless, we fall into the trap of genuinely believing that our anger is attributable to people or forces outside of ourselves. This way, we become victims of the cruelty of others or of circumstances, a person warranting empathy and understanding rather than the culprit who needs to take responsibility for their thoughts, words and actions.

People with this mentality betray themselves by venting their anger with 'you' statements like: 'You make me mad . . .' 'You infuriate me . . .' Their thought pattern goes something like this:

'You make me angry

So your action is responsible
For my feelings of pain.

So you are responsible
To make me feel right again.

So you must change
In the way I prescribe.

So I will resent you,
Reject you,
Force you to meet my demands
Until you shape up
And make things right.'[11]

'Blaming-anger of this kind is barren and impotent,'[12] claims David Augsburger. However costly the scene-shift seems to be, therefore, we need to make it so that we shed our martyr complex and face reality. We need to resolve to try to replace 'you' statements with 'I' statements like the following:

'I make me angry.

So your emotion or action
Does not control my reaction.

So I am responsible
For my feelings and actions.

So I cancel my demand
That you change as I prescribe.

So I will report
How I see you,
What I feel toward you,
Where I am in our differences,
What I am willing to do
In getting together again.'[13]

When we recognise, acknowledge and own our anger, we find ourselves curiously free both to feel its impact and to ask ourselves some pertinent questions whose answers may highlight ways that guarantee that we will grow through the experience rather than collapse under it. As we embark on these questions, there is great value, I find, in reminding myself, first of all, of a calming, objective truth, namely, that though it may seem as though God is far away from me he is, in fact, very near. Although my feelings may suggest that my world is hurtling out of control, the message they communicate is erroneous. God remains firmly in control. As the song puts it, God not only has the whole world in his hands, he has you and me in his hands. His care for each of us is unique, intimate and never-ending.

Over and over again, I have discovered that affirming this objective truth has stopped me in my tracks when rage or resentment have caused my spirit to crumble or when over-heated emotions have threatened to spiral out of control. With it comes a second reassurance that needs to be affirmed even though our feelings may mock, deride and question it: for some reason known only to himself, God has allowed this to happen; he has allowed it to happen to me.

When we have grasped and affirmed these truths, not only with our minds but in our experience, then we are in a position to process our anger creatively with the aid of a series of questions. By 'affirming these truths with our experience', I am thinking once again of the Dynamic Cycle of Being and Well-Being we looked at in chapter 2. When we are angry, whether rage or resentment has been triggered by a trivial remark or by an act as profoundly and deeply wounding as sexual harassment, we need, as much as we are able, to tuck the pain into God's heart. When I do this, I find that there, in that safe, loved, accepting place, God's presence, I can more quickly reach the heart of the problem: perceived rejection, felt vulnerability, dented pride and so on. In that reliable refuge, too, I sometimes hear God giving his perspective on the problem or assuring me that I am accepted and acceptable *with* the anger. God's nourishing acceptance provides the strength and resilience I need to confront the first question: 'What kind of anger is this that is consuming so much of my energy?' Is it rage that is bringing my blood to boiling point and convincing me that I have every right to attack and punish the offender? Is it resentment that, like a growling dog lurks in a shadowy corner of my heart looking for opportunities to leap on the offender and take its revenge? Or is it that Christlike response to unfairness and ungodliness: indignation?

If it is indignation that is consuming me, it quickly becomes clear what I must do: clear a space in my diary where, with God, I can look carefully at the injustice or ungodliness that is attracting my attention so that God can answer the cry of my heart: 'In the face of this injustice or crime, do you require anything of me? Is there some constructive way in which my energy may be channelled so that these wrongs may eventually be righted?'

If, however, I discern that it is rage or resentment that is rocking the boat of my life, the way ahead may not become so immediately obvious which is why I may need to address a few more questions like, 'What was it that triggered my anger this time?' and 'Is my anger justified?'

The reason why we need to ponder the second question is that anger, as we have seen, is an emotion that is triggered by something else. So, our anger may have been triggered, as Jesus' was, by injustice – in which case our response to the question, 'Is my anger justified?' will be a resounding 'yes'. Or our anger may have been triggered by the kind of compassion that tugged at Jesus' heart-strings when he watched people wandering around like sheep without a shepherd. In such instances, too, if we keep our ear close to his heart, God will be quick to assure us that our anger is indeed justified, that it can become a tool in his hands. On many occasions, though, our anger will have been triggered because we perceive that we have been slighted in some way. Maybe we have been overlooked, or ignored or eclipsed and our pride has been dented? The answer to the question, 'Is my anger justified?' then becomes patently plain and may give birth to a prayer that begs for God's help: 'Lord, deal with the taproot of my self-centredness. Free me to turn my back on self. Turn me, instead, to *your* praise and glory.'

An attitude that utters a prayer like that far-reaching one paves the way for facing three more questions:

'Is it worth expending so much energy on the situation that triggered my anger?';

'What purpose is my anger serving?';

'Do I want to control it or do I want its roots to burrow ever deeper into the soil of my heart?'

Controlling anger *is* possible if we decide we want to master it. As I said in an earlier chapter, think, for example, of the way we react if someone we like calls while we are arguing with a spouse, one of our children or someone who grates on us. Suddenly, our scowl is replaced by a smile. Suddenly the glare goes out of our eyes and they start to dance. Suddenly the harsh tone in our voice is replaced by warmth. The change is almost instant. Just as we find within ourselves the resources to change our behaviour in such circumstances, so we can change them in the absence of a visitor – if we want to; if we choose to. 'Controlling ourselves begins by deciding we want to control it; then moderating our behaviour will help. Speak softly: talking quietly has a calming effect on us, just as it will on the other person.'[14]

Before we are ready to process our anger in this thorough, demanding and life-changing way, other coping mechanisms might enable us to handle incensed feelings more effectively than in times past. Because anger is energy, for example, some people find it helpful deliberately to release the tension in a physical way: by mowing the lawn or cleaning the windows, playing squash or going for a vigorous walk, having a work-out in a swimming pool or gym – or even pounding a pillow. Others may need simply to rest, to unwind, to let the music of the sea or bird-song or a favourite song or chorus or instrumental wash over them until they feel calm and cleansed – ready to face head-on the potentially painful questions I have posed.

When we work through questions like these and find them beginning to yield their own answers, we may well find ourselves in the liberating position of feeling angry, yet being able to make creative choices. So, if someone, like one of our children or someone who dislikes us intensely sets out to irritate or hurt us, we can genuinely choose either to take the bait and retaliate or to refuse to react in the expected way and, instead, to make a considered response.

David Augsburger describes this unhooking with a personal illustration. Picture him driving along the highway with his wife. Absentmindedly, he misses the turning he had intended to take whereupon his wife observes, 'I'd have turned right back there.' He feels anger surging through his being. 'She's baiting me,' he mutters under his breath. 'She's hooking my anger and I'm too slow to interrupt'. Everything inside him wants to retaliate: 'I'd have turned right there too if I'd known then what we both know now.'

Later, he and his wife agree to re-run the sequence of events – to do the 'let's play it again' exercise. In this exercise, two or more people who have had an altercation reconstruct the incident in an attempt to establish what went wrong and why and, in order to learn and grow through the experience, to discover how they might each have acted differently. While they were doing this exercise, the proverbial penny dropped for the husband. It dropped when he realised that his wife never intended to bait him. After all, she was the passenger, he the driver. *She* wasn't watching for the intersection. He was. Only when his body language expressed the irritation he was feeling *with himself* did his wife make the innocent comment, 'I'd have turned right back there.' The penny drops again. 'You didn't bait me! I baited   you . . .' Tension evaporates. They laugh at themselves. Sometime later, when he misses a turning again, he chuckles and admits, 'I've just done it again!' 'We both laugh. We have reason to laugh . . . Owning your own anger . . . rather than blaming it on others, we can respond; we don't have to react. And there is a difference.'[15]

The Augsburgers are correct. We don't have to react, we can learn to respond. When we know we've han-

dled a situation badly, there is value in re-running it,
watching it play on the screens of our minds and learning   from it.

Communicate the primary feeling

There is value, too, in ensuring that, instead of pouring
out venom on someone with whom we are angry, we
seek to share with them the primary feeling that triggered off the anger. Let's use an imaginary marital
problem by way of illustration. Rita has been at home
all day with the children. Pete, her husband, has been
out of town on business but he promised to be home by
seven when they would enjoy a quiet, romantic meal
together. Rita baths the children early and has them in
bed early too. While the dinner cooks, she lays the
table, puts the candles in place and the wine in the
fridge. Seven approaches and as she brushes her hair,
she realises how much she is looking forward to spending quality time with Pete. Seven comes and there's no
sign of Pete. She silences her concern with a 'Never
mind! It's Friday. Perhaps he's got held up in traffic.'
Eight o'clock comes . . . eight-thirty . . . still no Pete. By
this time, she can no longer silence her fears. Her imagination runs riot: 'He's had an accident. He's been
killed'. She even wonders who will break the news to
her and wonders how she will cope with the children
on her own. At five past nine, when Pete eventually
arrives, instead of opening her arms to him, telling him
how worried she's been, how frightened she's been
that something dreadful had happened to him (the primary feeling of pain), how relieved she is to see him,
she lets rip: 'Where d'you think you've been? You
promised to be home at seven. And now it's after nine.
You're always late. You never put me first. I had the
dinner all ready – and now it's ruined.' And she bursts
into tears. Whereupon Pete, tired from a busy day at
work and from driving through nose-to-tail Friday

night traffic retaliates, meeting anger with anger. 'How d'you think *I* feel? I've been stuck in traffic for the past hour and a half. And I've had a busy day at work . . .' Not only is their meal ruined, but their evening is also. While the candles remain unlit on the table, they each go off in a huff and spend the rest of the evening in hostile silence. That night, as Pete creeps into bed, Rita seems to be sleeping. 'I'm really sorry,' Pete whispers. Rita, however, still full of resentment pretends to have fallen asleep. She chooses not to respond except by perpetuating the hostile silence. Resentment remains suppressed until an opportunity arises when it can seek revenge. Resentment strangles generosity and magnanimity. That is why, in circumstances like these, it is hard to become really vulnerable and to admit, 'I'm hurting . . .' But how different the evening could have been if Rita had said: 'I've been so worried . . .' Pete might then have taken her into his arms, held her, told her he loved her, apologised that he couldn't even phone her because the motorway traffic had been so heavy and then, even though the meal was past its best, it wouldn't have mattered. They would have been together with their mutual affection and understanding.

Recognise your natural tendency

Communicating the primary feeling is so difficult for most of us that we may need to do some spade work before we are able even to contemplate taking the risk. Part of the essential spadework is to recognise what we normally do with our anger when conflict erupts. Some people, for example, fight, like Rita. Some flee – literally. If Rita had been one of them, she would have stormed out of the house or gone to the bathroom or bedroom and locked the door. Some freeze – that is, they give one another 'the silent treatment'. As one man confessed to me on one occasion, when he and his wife reach deadlock over some issue or if they are angry with one another, 'we just don't speak to each other for a few days.' Giving one another the silent treatment, sulking, hiding one's feelings, putting up emotional barriers are all demonstrations of frozen rage – as serious and potentially dangerous as other ways of expressing anger. As Myra Chave-Jones warns us,

> Anger that is not expressed appropriately and con-structively does not just evaporate. These feelings will be smothered (and often buried more deeply) in the inner person, and gradually seep into our entire personality to make us bitter and twisted, and pos-sibly depressed. It may also leak into our bodies to help create an ulcer, arthritis, cancer or some similar condition.[16]

Learn the art of response-ability[17]

When we discover how we normally deal with rage or resentment, when we discern what our psychological reflex action is, we are then in a position to establish whether we are channelling these hyperactive emo-tions creatively or destructively. If we normally chan-nel them destructively, we are faced with a choice: to continue to behave in this way so that the potential of the anger is wasted in the same way as the potential of un-tended vines is wasted or to learn the art of taking responsibility – spelt response-ability. Harriet Goldhor Lerner defines response-ability in this way: it is 'the ability to observe ourselves and others in interaction and to respond to a familiar situation in a new and dif-ferent way. We cannot make another person change his or her steps to an old dance, but if we change our own step, the dance no longer can continue in the same pre-dictable pattern.'[18] In other words, learning response-ability involves not only seeking to understand why we react as we do but to go one step further – to determine when our natural response is the wisest one in the circumstances, to decide also whether an alternative response could have been more effective. We shall examine ways of doing this in the next chapter. Before you read on, however, again it might prove helpful to pause and to reflect on some of your responses to the content of *this* chapter; to think through some of the following questions.

Suggested exercises

1. Think of an occasion when you were angry. What was the primary emotion that gave birth to the anger? In retrospect, what warning do you think the anger was trying to give you? With that incident in mind, how would you respond to the following questions:
- What kind of anger was it: rage, resentment or indignation?
- What triggered the powerful reaction?
- What, in particular, was it that induced such a strong reaction?
- What was the real issue? What was the nub of the matter?
- Whose problem was it – yours or someone else's?
- What, specifically, do you want to change?
- What makes it difficult for people to communicate the primary emotion?
- What makes it difficult for you to communicate the primary emotion rather than the rage?

2. In *Love and Anger in Marriage*, David Mace describes how he used to feel when he became angry with his wife:

I was aware of a rapidly developing state of tension.

Somewhere in my chest, or down in the pit of my stomach, I felt a tangled knot that was giving me pain. There seemed to be a rapidly accumulating mass of hot, poisonous material somewhere inside me. I was not conscious of any urge to attack Vera physically, but I was certainly clenching my fists and trying to keep myself under control. At the same time I was aware of a devastating sense of alienation and disillusionment because I was actually feeling hate toward the person I wanted, of all people in the world, to love. My overwhelming urge was to disengage, to get away – out of Vera's presence – so that I could somehow deal with these frightening emotions which she seemed to be generating in me. My whole world seemed to be collapsing, and my impelling urge was to escape, to hide somewhere until I could begin to cope with the tumult within me.[19]

What happens to you physically, emotionally and spiritually when you are angry? (It might help to put your thoughts in writing as David Mace did.)

3. How do you feel when you see someone else who is angry – that is, how do you feel about the person and how do you feel about the rage or the resentment or the indignation? Do you secretly condemn the person and seek to distance yourself from them or can you offer them acceptance by quietly praying for them, listening to them, genuinely attempting to understand why they are in such turmoil, seeking to hear the primary emotion that is giving rise to the outburst? Do you communicate coldness and rejection or the kind of compassion and tenderness, respect and desire to help God gives you when you are angry?

4. Do you feel more comfortable with indignation,

with resentment or rage? Do you know why?

5. How do you feel when someone is angry with you?

6. When you are angry, do you fight, take flight or freeze? Do you always react in the same way or does your reaction vary? Do you, for example:

• Withdraw into yourself?

• Find it hard to admit, even to yourself, 'I'm angry'

• Recognise that you are angry and pause to make a calculated choice asking yourself, 'What will I do with this anger?'
  – punish the person I'm angry with
  – admit that I'm angry and ask for help with the underlying hurt or fear
  – suggest to the person concerned that we talk about the situation that triggered the anger when we have both had time to process it
  – put yourself in the other person's shoes in an attempt to understand how he or she is feeling; where he or she is coming from
  – make a calculated choice to channel the energy so that the conflict works for the good of the relationship
  – accuse the other person of making you angry instead of reminding yourself that no one can make you angry. They can, at most, trigger a reaction

7. Would you like to change the way you process anger? If so, what changes would you like to make? Tell God about them. Give God an opportunity to respond.

8. Reflect on the following:

'A gentle answer turns away wrath,
but a harsh word stirs up anger.'

(Prov 15:1)

'A fool gives full vent to his anger,
but a wise man keeps himself under control.'
(Prov 29:11)

'Stirring up anger produces strife.'
(Prov 30:33)

Write a prayer in response to your reflections.

PART 3

Dealing With Conflict

7

Taking Response-ability

Immediately after finishing chapter 6 of this book, I went for a walk by the beach near my home. The sun shone warm on my face, an onshore breeze ruffled my hair, the golden corn swayed first this way, then that. While I was drinking in the sheer wonder of it all, a tree stopped me in my tracks – a stark, naked, leafless fig tree that stood silhouetted against the gentian blue sea. The tree's trunk was silver. Its branches looked like arms upstretched in worship. Each arm clutched little clusters of new green figs that looked like clumps of brussels sprouts. How on earth have they managed to grow? I asked myself. Didn't those howling gales and raging seas of the past few weeks deter them? Obviously not. Such is the way of nature.

For hours, the mental photograph I had taken of that tree impressed itself on my mind. It became a parable for me reminding me that, no matter how adverse or stressful our circumstances, even though we may be stripped of everything: our dignity, our loved ones, our possessions, our health, we, too, can bear luscious new fruit.

Towards the end of the last chapter, I mentioned one such fruit: the fruit of learning response-ability. We noted that response-ability is the skill of observing ourselves and others as we seek to relate to each other, and where necessary, to respond to familiar situations in new and different ways. As we observed in an earlier chapter of the book, it is virtually impossible to change another's pattern of behaviour without wounding them. We *can*, however, change our own responses to another's behaviour in such a way that the dynamic of the relationship gradually changes. We usually make the necessary changes painfully slowly and with a great deal of difficulty because unpicking old behaviour patterns is even more painstaking than unpicking a knitted garment. But it can be done.

Our task in this chapter, then, is threefold. The first is to seek to take an objective look at some of the ways people react to conflict. The second is to treat this information as though it were a mirror in which we can see a reflection of our normal way of behaving. The third is to assess where our instinctive, preferred method of reacting to conflict is the most appropriate and where an alternative response might replace havoc with harmony.

Some effects of conflict

Different people react to conflict in different ways. I was reminded of this while leading a group discussion on one occasion. For most of the evening, relationships in the group had been happy and harmonious. Members of the group were each contributing to the discussion in a helpful, integrative way. As each handed over pieces of the verbal jigsaw, a complete picture began to emerge. Towards the end of the meeting, however, quite out the blue, someone asked a provocative question. The question plunged us into a theological controversy that triggered an outburst from a woman sitting on the opposite side of the room from the questioner. The smile disappeared from this woman's face and was replaced by a scowl. Her voice became strident and succeeded in bringing all discussion to an abrupt halt. The atmosphere in the group changed dramatically. Discord seemed to resonate right round the room.

The reactions of different members of the group

intrigued me. Some moved to the edge of their seats as though they relished the idea of a verbal ding-dong. Others inched deeper and deeper into their armchairs as though they wanted to hide. More than a few looked confused, embarrassed and alarmed. Mounting tension prompted some to clench their fists and others to screw up their eyes as though they were praying a desperate one-word prayer, 'Help!'

Mercifully, this particular verbal bomb was defused quickly and harmlessly. The reflex actions I had observed reminded me, though, that the group had teetered on the brink of an emotional Hiroshima. We had been given a timely reminder that conflict in relationships can spark off aggression, defensiveness, criticism, insecurity, division, mistrust, pretence, avoidance and a whole host of other emotions and reactions.

Although conflict is common, its body blows are rarely soft. As David Cormack reminds us, when conflict assaults us, 'we lose peace; we lose confidence; we lose sleep; we lose health, and eventually – if the inner struggles are not checked – we may lose our sanity and our very life.'[1] He continues: 'Conflict affects our attitudes . . . our activities and our hopes.'[2] Conflict gives rise to suspicion, 'suspicion leads to fear, fear to violence, violence to more violence. In marriages, in industry, in racial and religious intolerance – in cities, in neighbourhoods, in churches and families – the process is the same: conflict feeds conflict.'[3]

Conflict can also generate fear, sap us of emotional energy, and, since it affects our relationship with God, deplete our spiritual resources also. As we saw in chapter 4, conflict paralyses some personality types so deeply that the whole of life is adversely affected. It can lead to serious disorders like anxiety attacks and depression. That is why it is essential that we recognise and evaluate some of the ways different people react to discord.

Placating

A number of studies have been made into this phenomenon. The consequent consensus of opinion appears to be that, by and large, most people prefer one of five options. Their choice is determined by two main factors: whether they are more goal-oriented than relationship-centred or whether relationships mean more to them than achieving their goals.

David Augsburger in *Caring Enough to Confront* summarises the situation helpfully. He asserts that, when faced with conflict, some people almost always give in to the person they are in conflict with. Their concern for their relationship with that person rates so highly in their estimation and their interest in achieving their own goals assumes such a low priority in their lives that they almost always yield. In diagrammatic terms, this thinking looks like this:

Increasing concern for good relationships ↑

YIELDERS
Give in
Smooth over
Accomodate

RESOLVERS
Seek a solution
Collaborate
Lasting synthesis of interests

COMPROMISERS
Win-a-little
Lose-a-little
Temporary balance of interests

AVOIDERS
Withdraw

COMPETITORS
Compete to win
Force a showdown

Increasing concern for personal goals, ideals, values and ideas

Reactions to Conflict[4]

A woman who could arguably be considered the patron saint of 'yielders' came into my life when she and her husband attended a marriage seminar my husband and I were leading. When I introduced the subject of marital conflict at the beginning of the day, this woman's husband retorted: 'My wife and I *never* quarrel.' I looked at his wife as though to ask whether she wanted to respond whereupon, in a quiet voice, she agreed: 'Yes. That's right. We never quarrel.'

I found myself strangely disturbed by this couple's confession but pressed on with the material I had prepared for the group.

The day went well. The level of trust between the handful of couples present visibly rose as time wore on so, at the end of the day, my husband and I invited the couples to share with the group thoughts or insights that had made an impact on them or resolutions they had made. The last person to speak was this 'patron saint of yielders'. In her quiet, hesitant way she confessed: 'I realised today that my husband and I were being quite honest when we said we never quarrelled. We don't. But the reason *why* we never quarrel is that, whenever there's any conflict around, I immediately give in.'

'*I give in*' – that's the key. This woman almost always 'loses' in a conflict situation with her husband. She loses because she yields. She yields because she is dependent on him and therefore needs to placate him. She not only placates him, she seeks to smooth over the creases that even a hint of conflict creates in their relationship.

David and Frank Johnson, in their fascinating study of ways in which individuals react to friction, liken people who fall into this category to teddy bears. They seek to preserve the relationship at all costs because they want to be accepted and liked. They fear that conflict cannot be discussed without damaging relationships and so they avoid conflict in rather the same way

as most people avoid AIDS – and for the same reason;
because they are terrified that if conflict invades their
relationship, someone will be seriously hurt and their
relationship ruined.

I sometimes liken people in this category to pet poodles. I think of two poodles I often meet when I am
walking near the village where I stay when I am visiting England. Meekly they trot beside their owner wearing a different coat according to the season – a tartan
one in summer, for example and a sheepskin one in
winter. They seem to exist to please their owner who
has taught them to sit up and beg, to shake a paw and
to curl up on his lap like purring cats.

Whether we liken them to teddy bears or pet poodles matters little. The relevant piece of information to
remember is that people in this category communicate,
by implication, that their motto goes something like
this: '*My* goals don't matter. I'll give them all up. I'll let
you have what you want because then, perhaps, you'll
like me.'

Competing to win

In the opposite corner to yielders – or placators as some
people call them – sit the competitors. Goals are of such
great importance to competitors that they seek to reach
the target no matter what it costs. Competitors compete
for one reason – to win. Their overriding need to climb
to the top of the ladder persuades them, where necessary, to attack, overpower, overwhelm and intimidate
others (verbally, if not physically). When they have
succeeded in winning an argument, or some other contest, they glow with pride and the consequent sense of
achievement. Conversely, when they lose, they collapse from the consequent shame and sense of inadequacy and failure. Because they are so fiercely task-oriented, their philosophy is that if winning is at the
expense of others, so be it. They are prepared to sacrifice relationships if this is the price that has to be paid

for remaining in control. They must win – others must lose.

I sometimes liken competitors to the proverbial bull-in-a-china shop. They know what they want and, no matter what obstacle is in the way, if necessary, they will trample on it and crush it.

I once watched two such people compete in Dubai airport. We had been fellow passengers on the plane that had brought us to Dubai and we had travelled all night. It was now five in the morning. We were tired; each living on a short fuse. Even so, their competitiveness had me all agog. We were transit passengers and had been instructed to go to a certain part of the airport to have our passports checked. One competitor (competitor number one) went, at first, to the wrong place where he was first in the queue. When he realised his mistake, he moved to the correct queue and assumed that he could be first in line there also. But another man (competitor number two) headed this queue. Nevertheless, competitor number one pushed in and, standing in front of competitor two, claimed in an aggressive, authoritarian tone of voice: 'I was here before you. I *know* because I watched you arrive – but I'd been told to queue in the wrong place. Still, I was first, so this is *my* place'. Number two drew himself up to his full height and made it abundantly clear that he did not intend to stand for this kind of nonsense. He proceeded to elbow competitor number one out of the queue, whereupon number one raised his voice in protest. Number two flushed with rage and retorted angrily: 'Well! That's your problem. I'm here and I'm staying . . .' They hurled abuse at one another, threatened each other and almost came to blows. I am not a competitor and could scarcely believe my eyes and ears. *Why*, I kept asking myself, are they kicking up such a fuss at this time in the morning? Since there were only five of us in the queue anyway, it seemed to me incomprehensible that two grown men could work up such a head of steam over something as trivial as being first in such a short line.

Compromising

The competitor's motto is 'I must win. You must lose.' I wonder what a third category of person, a compromiser, would have made of the competitors' stand-up row? While placators expect to lose in a conflict situation and competitors determine to win each and every contest, compromisers skilfully scheme to win a little and lose a little. Goals are moderately important to them. Relationships are equally important. When faced with disharmony or a clash of viewpoints, they are therefore prepared to concede a little so long as those who think differently from themselves are also prepared to opt for a little give-and-take. To achieve this win-a-little, lose-a-little goal, compromisers can become self-assertive and manipulative. They can also be gently persuasive, affable and flexible. Their motto is: 'Let's all place our personal desires into the common pool for the good of the community. This way everyone becomes a winner.'

There is a sense in which most of us have to be compromisers for much of the time. I think, for example, of the retreats that my husband and I sometimes lead. People come to them bringing such very different needs and expectations. Some beg to have meals in silence. Others make it quite plain that silent meals, for them, seem nonsensical. Some want to sing at the beginning of most meetings. Others prefer to listen to quiet, contemplative music. And so on. For the compromisers, the variety of expectations expressed pose no problems whatsoever. Others, however, can feel alienated by such a wide range of hopes and likes and dislikes.

Avoiding

While compromisers busily attempt to create harmony,

yet another group of people, the conflict-avoiders, react to tensions in an entirely different way. Having little concern either for goals or relationships, they are prepared to relinquish both. When conflict erupts, they therefore withdraw and abdicate all responsibility. Conflict-avoiders are the people who, in that group I mentioned earlier in this chapter, inched themselves deeper and deeper into their armchairs as though they hoped the chair would swallow them up or at least act as a camouflage. Conflict-avoiders feel helpless when people disagree. Believing that trying to resolve the problem is but a futile exercise, they feel utterly helpless and consequently withdraw, where at all possible, from people they are at variance with. Some physically walk or storm out of a room if conflict breaks out. Others withdraw into themselves, leaving the room and the discussion psychologically by switching off. Conflict-avoiders are almost always passive, non-assertive, shrug-their-shoulders, phlegmatic type of people. Their motto is, 'If I'm uncomfortable or can't cope, I quit. If I leave, I lose but that's better than staying and losing.'

I sometimes liken conflict-avoiders to hedgehogs. I think of the one that attracted my attention during supper when I was on retreat on one occasion. It had become ensnared in the nets that were protecting the raspberry canes from birds. In a desperate, last-ditch attempt to extricate itself, it was struggling so violently that the net looked as though it was jumping up and down. As soon as supper was over, a friend and I mounted a rescue operation. Taking a pair of scissors, we snipped the section of the net that was trapping the creature's little body and my friend gently lifted it out of its prison and carried it to freedom. Whereupon the hedgehog curled up into a tight ball and pushed out its prickles. We talked to it. It didn't budge. We brought it milk. Still it didn't move. It had completely and in doing so denied itself the milk it might have enjoyed.

Conflict-avoiders are like that. Fear prompts them to flee or to hide robbing them of the benefits of conflict.

Resolving

In the opposite corner from the avoiders, we find the conflict-resolvers. Goals and relationships are rated equally highly by such people. Consequently, they view conflicts in a very different way from conflict-avoiders. Conflict, for them, has a smiling face. 'There are no such things as problems, only opportunities,' they claim. Their aim, when conflict peeps around the corner, is to seek a solution that enables them and the other person to achieve their goals. They believe that conflict can be the counsellor that points the way to the enrichment of relationships, the friend who helps to reduce tension between two or more people. They introduce into the conflict arena objective, amicable discussion that seeks to pin-point and define the problem. They refuse to rest until a satisfactory solution has been found and until all tensions, misunderstandings and animosity have been cleared up.

Before we go on to ask the question so many people pose: 'Which response is right?' we need to acknowledge one other approach to the kind of clashes we have been considering in this book so far – conflict-excluding. David and Vera Mace mention this response when writing for married couples. The conflict-excluding couple, they suggest, looks rather like this:

One appears larger than the other. Psychologically, he or she is bigger. Conflict-excluders set out to control relationships and groups in such a way that they prevent clashes by putting an embargo on a whole variety of topics that threaten their *raison d'être*. What excluders fail to recognise is that, though they attempt to rule out conflict, they create it simply by being who they are – dominant, controlling people.

The placator I mentioned earlier in this chapter was married to an excluder. Maybe she had become a placator *because* she had married a forceful, dominating husband? That is not to say that, when conflict erupts, we should never yield. Clearly there are times when to give in is the most constructive way forward.

Giving in

When, for example, it becomes clear that we are wrong, if we are to keep our integrity, we must give in. Or, when we know that any influence we may have in a given situation is minimal, again, the wisest course of action might well be to capitulate. There are times, too, when we may sense that maintaining harmony matters more than anything else at this point in time and that maintaining it is best achieved by yielding. Then, of course, giving in could be our unique gift to a sensitive situation. Equally, there are times when we perceive that the person with whom we are sparring needs to learn from their mistakes. Here again, giving in may be the wisest, most effective, most powerful response we can make in the circumstances.

One of the most memorable examples in history of the appropriateness in certain circumstances of yielding is the role his mother played in the conversion of St Augustine. Monica goes down in history as one of the most prayerful mothers the world has ever known. In his *Confessions* Augustine testifies to the way she prayed for him while he was being formed in her womb, prayed for him, too, when he was sick as a child and taught him to pray for himself. He, however, refused to follow in her footsteps. From an early age he kicked over the traces, lying to his parents as well as stealing from them and others. By the age of sixteen, the brambles of lust had grown high over his head, as he, himself, colourfully describes his lifestyle. Like the woman of her culture that she was, his mother exerted enormous pressure on her son to keep on the straight and narrow. Augustine, however, refused. Like the prodigal son in Jesus' parable, his mind was made up and nothing could deter him. He would live life his own way.

Monica had no alternative but to capitulate.

In the circumstances, yielding proved to be the wisest, most effective, most powerful choice she could possibly have made. When she let go of her son (except through prayer), God took over. 'Pick up and read, pick up and read,' God eventually whispered to Augustine one unforgettable day. Recognising the voice as God's, Augustine seized the copy of the Scriptures he had been reading in the garden. The verse that leapt off the page read: 'Not in revelling and drunkenness, not in lust and wantonness, not in quarrels and rivalries. Rather arm yourselves with the Lord Jesus Christ: spend no more thought on nature and nature's appetites' (Rom 13:13–14). Augustine recalls how, 'In an instant, as I came to the end of the sentence, it was as though the light of confidence flooded into my heart and all the darkness of doubt was dispelled.'[5] As for Monica, she was reunited with her much-loved son with whom she spent the final months of her life in blissful companionship and with whom she sipped the elixir of being immersed in God's felt love.

Competing and withdrawing

Similarly, in certain circumstances, competing could be the most effective plan of campaign. Think, for example, of those occasions when a group needs to make a swift decision. Time is short, a competitive type has access to vital facts that others do not have access to, others in the group are slow thinkers who need time to process facts and figures even when they have them. Then it could well be right for a competitive type to take control of that part of the meeting and almost appear to steamroller it. Most members of the group would not only see the wisdom of such a course of action, they would be grateful for the competitor's quick-mindedness.

At the opposite extreme, there are occasions when to withdraw can be the most constructive way to proceed. There are times, for example, when we have no power so there seems little point in expending time and energy on confronting the issues at stake. There are other occasions when the matter in question seems so trivial that, again, it hardly seems worth spending the time and energy debating or arguing about it. And there are other reasons for withdrawing. A friend of mine explained one to a gathering of bishops and clergy in Tanzania on one occasion. He was speaking to them on the subject of conflict in the home. They were drinking in every word – both the English in which my friend addressed them and the interpretation which was being beautifully given by one of the bishops. When the speaker confessed, 'There are times when I feel so angry with my children that I have to say to them, "I can't discipline you now because I'm too angry with you, I must wait until my anger cools down, then I'll discipline you," ' the interpreter paused instead of speaking straight away. As I watched him, I noticed that he was fighting back a torrent of tears. Making a monumental effort, he translated into Swahili the words that had been spoken: 'There are times when I feel so angry with my children that I have to say to them, "I can't discipline you now because I'm too angry with you . . ." ' Overflowing now with emotion, his voice trailed away and he sat down at the table on the platform, buried his head in his hands and wept. The speaker sat down beside him. Interpreter and speaker suddenly had become icons of integrity, totally vulnerable. There is power in vulnerability. Not surprisingly, then, a powerful hush now descended on the gathering. Glancing round the auditorium, tears flowed from my heart into my eyes also. Most of the other bishops and clergy were quietly weeping. It was as though the Holy Spirit was penetrating our armour and emphasising that, indeed, there are times when the surge of anger rising in us is so strong that we need to withdraw until that red hot rage has had time to go off the boil.

There are other occasions when we need to look at a situation subjectively as well as objectively. If we merely look at it objectively, applying to it theories and facts, it might seem as though confrontation is essential. If, however, we take people and their feelings and their emotional well-being into consideration, we might reach a very different conclusion. Instead of confronting, we might well withdraw.

I think of an occasion when a friend of mine was speaking at a certain conference where she came under attack from the person who was leading the worship. Together with her husband and the worship-leader's wife, she met her attacker to try to get to the bottom of the animosity and distrust that seemed to divide them. To her dismay, however, the worship leader used the meeting to bombard her with yet more criticism. Feeling humiliated and crushed, she heard herself say, 'I'm sorry but I don't feel there's any point in continuing with this meeting,' whereupon she walked out of the room.

'I've never done such a thing in my life before,' she confessed to me. 'Whatever made me do it?' Eventually, after she had worked through the guilt and the self-blame with which she was riddled, she unearthed the real reason. 'I did it for his wife's sake,' she admitted. 'She'd been coming to me for coun-selling. I know how fragile she is. I know that if I'd con-fronted him in the way I wanted to, this could have really wounded her further. Suddenly I felt so helpless, so hopeless, so angry at his insensitivity to his own wife's needs, let alone to my feelings. Something inside me snapped and I fled from the room.'

While I have been writing this chapter, I have been processing occasions when I noticed how, though I remained in the room with them, I had been with-drawing psychologically from a certain couple's con-versation. 'What made me react in this way?' I've asked myself umpteen times.

The clue came when I heard myself say to a friend, 'In some ways the man is just like my father . . .' My father was a godly man for whom I thank God fre-quently. Like the rest of us, though, he was far from perfect. One of his weaknesses was that when he had a fixed idea in his head, nothing and no one could per-suade him that there might be another way of looking at the subject under discussion. I would listen to him argue the toss with others yet refuse to concede that there could be another way of seeing things. And I would be embarrassed. When confronted with my father's rock-solid rigidity as a teenager and as a young adult, I discovered that the simplest solution to the problem was to withdraw. Now, here I am, faced with a similar scenario and still I withdraw because, as David Cormack puts it: 'When people have fixed ideas, when dogma, doctrine and desire become absolute, immutable and "truth", then the immovable becomes unteachable, and the unteachable becomes the bigot, and the bigot will man any barricade in defence of his ignorance.'[6]

Suggested exercises

1. Our task in the next chapter is to seek to understand what is involved in becoming a conflict-
resolver. Before moving on, however, I recommend
that readers imagine that the diagram on p   is a mirror. Bearing in mind the contents of this chapter,
gaze into the mirror until you see yourself reflected
in it. In other words, seek to discover what your reg-
ular reactions to conflict are.

2. Different people react to conflict in different ways
and at different times. Just because we normally
withdraw as soon as we sniff conflict, that doesn't
necessarily mean that we shall always behave in this
way. So try to think of occasions when you *have*
withdrawn. Then try to assess the reasons why you
withdrew. Was it because you feel that differences
are intrinsically wrong? Was it because the
inevitability of differences daunts you? Was it
because you believed that nothing would be
achieved by staying? Or was there another reason?

3. Next try to remember an occasion when you acted
as though you were a competitor. Did you determine to win like those two men at the airport? If so,
do you remember why? Was it because you were
convinced you were right? Was it because you
believed that the differences needed to be erased?
Or was there some other reason?

4. Have you ever reacted in the way a placator
behaves? If so, relive the memory before asking
yourself some more questions. Did you behave in
this particular way because you believe that differences drive wedges between people? Did you react
in this way because you believe that differences con-
stitute personal attacks on people? Or did you

respond in this way because you believe that conflict demands sacrifice from someone and the willingness to yield? Maybe there was some other reason?

5. Next, think back to occasions when you have compromised. What happened? How did you feel when you relinquished some of your cherished hopes for the common cause? Would you say you are more goal-oriented than people-centred or vice-versa?

6. Complete the following Responding to Conflict questionnaire:

Reflect on these possible responses to clashes with another person. Place an x beside the 10 statements that best describe your responses to disagreement or disharmony. Place two xx against the most frequent responses. As you do the exercise, try to focus on a specific clash of some kind in which you have been embroiled and bear in mind that, the more honest you are the more you will discover about yourself.

1. Withdraw into yourself

2. Negotiate/compromise

3. Try to talk with the person concerned

4. Give in

5. Force your own way

6. Become a 'martyr'

7. Exaggerate or overstate the problem

8. Clarify the issue with clear statements

9. Go silent

10. Hide your real feelings

11. Use sarcasm or criticism

12. Blame: 'you never . . .'; 'You always. . . '

13. Evade the issue

14. Stop when you seem to be losing the argument

15. Agree to differ

16. Use threatening language or emotional blackmail

17. Threaten the person physically

18. Try to understand the point of view

19. Pretend the problem doesn't exist

20. Explore openly each side of the issue
21. Become resentful
22. Leave the room: walk away

23. Use a number of 'I' statements

24. Use a number of 'You' statements

25. Share your feelings

26. Refuse to discuss the issue at all

27. Try to work out a compromise

28. Disappear for a while (hoping the problem will disappear too)

29. Procrastinate/stall/be too busy to talk

30. Work towards a just resolution of the conflict

Now reflect on the implications of your responses:

My attitude is:

I win/you win:	I compete to win:
I value you and affirm you	I don't value or affirm you
I am saying 'I win and you win'	I am demanding 'I win and you lose'

2. Negotiate	3. Out-talk
8. Clarify	5. Force
15. Agree to differ	7. Exaggerate
18. Try to understand	11. Criticise. Be sarcastic
20. Explore	12. Blame
23. Use 'I' statements	16. Physical treatment
25. Share feelings	17. Emotional threat
27. Compromise	24. Use 'You' statements
30. Resolution	

I placate	I avoid
Defer 'I lose and you win'	Defect 'I lose and you lose'

4. Give in	1. Withdraw
6. Act martyrlike	13. Evade
9. Go silent	14. Stop if losing
10. Hide feelings	22. Leave the room
19. Pretend	26. Refuse discussion
21. Resentful	29. Procrastinate[7]

- Are your responses really responses or are they reactions?
- How often does your considered response differ from your off-the-cuff reaction?
- Are there changes you would like to make?
- If so, how would you like to change?
- What kind of help might you need to enable you to make these changes?

8

SEEKING RECONCILIATION

When conflict erupts, different people react to it in different ways. Some fiercely compete with one another, others recoil from each other and yet others seek a compromise. As an incentive to embark on some personal stock-taking that will result in us learning the art of response-ability, these are the observations we examined in detail in chapter 7. In *Peacing Together*, however, David Cormack makes this passionate plea: 'What our society needs now is not more avoidance, more compromise or more competition. What we need now is more reconciliation – fewer sword-bearers and more peacemakers.'[1]

Within minutes of copying out that quotation, I met a friend who poured out the anguish she feels over what is happening in the church she used to attend. One vicar has left, another has arrived, the ministry of the fellowship has changed dramatically and, as a result, scores of people have left this fellowship that once pulsated with life. The conversation reminded me of the many, many fellowships that have split – not once, but several times. I was reminded, too, of the sadness I felt when one church team confessed to me not long before I started this manuscript, 'We've reached complete deadlock and we don't know what to do. We've tried everything we can think of but still there's this terrible stalemate.' With these and other memories swirling round my mind, I felt convinced that David Cormack had hit the nail right on the head.

An hour or so after the conversation I have just mentioned, I 'happened' to be reading John 13. The context
is that bitter-sweet meal, the Last Supper. Jesus has
expressed his unique love for each of his disciples by
washing, then wiping their soiled feet. While the memory of the tenderness with which he had wiped
between their toes was still fresh in their minds, he
gave them a mandate for the future:

'You call me 'Teacher' and 'Lord', and rightly so, for
that is what I am. Now that I, your Lord and Teacher,
have washed your feet, you also should wash one
another's feet. I have set you an example that you
should do as I have done for you' (John 13:13–15). A little later, as though to reinforce this message, he hands
them another challenge: 'Love one another. *As I have
loved you*, so you must love one another' (John 13:34,
emphasis mine).

'We all know these words by heart,' I reasoned to
myself. 'We sing them with one breath and curse each
other with the next.' I then 'happened' to read 2
Corinthians 5. There it was again – that same mandate.
Only this time it is Paul who is insisting that believers
have been entrusted with a very special and costly ministry – the ministry of reconciliation:

'God . . . reconciled us to himself through Christ and
gave us the ministry of reconciliation' (2 Cor 5:18, emphasis mine).

Or, as Eugene Peterson paraphrases this dynamic,
revolutionary, far-reaching verse:

'God . . . settled the relationship between us and
him, *and then called us to settle our relationships with each
other . . . We're Christ's representatives. God uses us to
persuade men and women to drop their differences and enter
into God's work of making things right between them*' (vv
18,19, *The Message*, emphasis mine).

The meaning of reconciliation

Why, I wondered, have we not taken these exhortations more seriously? Why is it now almost fashionable to be at variance with fellow Christians or friends or members of one's own family? Is it because the cost to our own person of becoming one of God's instruments of peace and reconciliation is so high that we shrink from this ministry rather than accepting it with gratitude? Possibly. To become a reconciler, after all, might cost us not less than everything. Think of Jesus, for example. In reconciling us to God, he poured out his life-blood – and died in the process. Or think of Zacchaeus. In seeking reconciliation with those he had robbed, this one-time extortioner lost much of his wealth as well as losing face. Losses of this magnitude are seemingly inevitable. The Greek word Paul uses for reconciliation is *katalasso* which means 'to change mutually' or 'to change completely'. In other words, reconciliation has as its goal relationships that are changed through and through; completely changed. Few changes take place without pain.

The *Pocket Oxford Dictionary* helps us to understand why pain and change go together. As a definition of the verb 'to reconcile' it suggests: 'to make friendly after an estrangement, harmonise, make compatible, show compatibility of'. If *we* are to become one of the world's reconcilers, whenever we find ourselves locked in conflict with someone, our aim should therefore be to pursue peace and unity while shunning division, to create harmony rather than to add to discord, to seek a solution rather than to contribute to strife, to flesh out that immortal prayer attributed to Francis of Assisi:

Lord make me an instrument of your peace;
Where there is hatred, let me sow love.
Where there is injury, pardon;
Where there is discord, unity;

Where there is error, truth;
Where there is doubt, faith;
Where there is despair, hope;
Where there is darkness, light;
Where there is sadness, joy.

O divine Master,
grant that I may not so much seek to be consoled
    as to console;
to be understood as to understand;
to be loved, as to love;
for it is in giving that we receive,
it is in pardoning that we are pardoned,
and it is in dying that we are born to eternal life.[2]

An example

In *Love and Anger in Marriage*, David and Vera Mace
have shown us that such reconciliation is possible.
Describing their marriage, David Mace writes: 'Vera
and I are now in our forty-ninth year of marriage . . .
We would unhesitatingly rate our marriage as a happy
one, and I believe our closest friends would concur in
that judgement.'[3]

He goes on, however, to describe the sense of disillusionment and alienation that he experienced when,
in the early days of their marriage, conflict prised them
apart. He was a self-confessed withdrawer. His overwhelming urge, when they had quarrelled, was to
escape from Vera's presence so that he could deal with
the hatred that consumed him as he thought of her.
Without explaining to Vera what he was doing or
where he was going, he *did* escape. 'Then, in isolation,
I would try to calm my confused and heated emotions,
striving to see the incident in clearer perspective and to
balance it out with more positive feelings. As time
passed, I would slowly calm down, get myself tidied

up, and then return in the hope that our original good relationship could be restored.'[4]

Vera recalls that David would sometimes disappear for long stretches of time. Sometimes she could guess why her husband had absented himself. At other times, though, she simply had no idea where he was or what he was doing. She consequently concluded that she had married a very moody man. When David returned, she longed to talk to him about the conflict but feared to do so lest she should 'rock the boat'.

Because they were determined to become conflict-resolvers rather than conflict-avoiders, they agreed to make a study of the subject of anger and how best to process it. And, in their determination to find a solution to their painful, recurring problem, they experimented with a variety of ways of changing their behaviour patterns. Eventually, after much trial and error, they found a solution that worked for them and that has worked for countless couples and teams ever since. They entered into a contract with one another that they called a three-step plan.

Step one We agreed that we would communicate our states of anger to each other as soon as possible, and hopefully before they could lead to unpleasant consequences. This was based on our conviction that anger was a healthy emotion which was trying to tell us something about ourselves and our relationship. We accepted as perfectly normal the fact that in a close relationship, we would from time to time get angry with each other, and we gave each other full and free permission to do so. That really cleared the air and freed us from guilt.

Step two We made a pledge to each other that while it was O.K. to be angry, it was definitely not O.K. to attack the other in response to that anger. We saw that no gain of any kind could come from launching an attack . . . We saw the venting of anger as a psychological equivalent of spitting and we saw no justification for this between people trying to develop a loving relationship.

Step three We made a contract that every anger situation that threatened our relationship would be worked through by both of us and owned by both of us, not as a personal weakness in the one who was angry, but as a function of our total relationship. In step three, the angry person requested help, and the one toward whom the anger was being directed gave assurance of a response . . . We adopted a policy that every anger situation between us was in fact an opportunity for growth in our relationship and must be dealt with accordingly – otherwise, we were missing a valuable chance to achieve a deeper understanding of ourselves and of each other. In other words, anger is not something evil to be avoided or suppressed. It is not even something inconvenient to be disposed of so that we can get back to the business of living. It is, properly understood, raw material to be used in the positive development of a better and more secure relationship.[5]

Over a period of time, as they honoured their commitment to one another, they ceased to be alarmed when anger threatened their marriage because they steadily gained in confidence that they could handle it. They were, after all, working hard at adjusting their behaviour as well as attempting to interpret accurately the actions and reactions of the other. In working at this area of their marriage that had created so much division, they were both exercising their God-given ministry of reconciliation.

Be assertive

It takes courage to draw up a contract like the Mace's drew up. It takes even more courage to honour it. It not only takes courage, it demands of both partners that they become assertive. The word 'assertive' is one that is easily misunderstood because it has been hi-jacked in recent years by those who believe 'assertion' to be synonymous with 'aggression'. 'Assertion' needs, therefore, to be carefully defined. David Cormack defines it well:

> 'Assertion' describes our behaviour when we seek to achieve or express our own needs, opinions, feelings and beliefs in a direct, open and honest way and at the same time seek to encourage the reciprocal expression by the other party. We recognise that we have rights to be met, and that those around us also have rights we should be seeking to ensure are met. Assertion recognises that we *are* our brother's keepers. We all have rights. We have rights that come from the laws of the land; we have rights that come from the policies and practices of the organisation in which we work and serve; we have rights that come from our human identity – in the fact that we are made in the image of the infinite God.[6]

One of the most moving expressions of assertion I have ever heard came from the lips of a close friend of mine while we were on holiday together on one occasion. My friend and I are very similar in temperament, share similar priorities, enjoy being together and understand one another well. On this occasion, though, a misunderstanding had prompted me to withdraw to lick my wounds. While I curled into a prickly ball like the hedgehog I described in chapter 7, my friend felt completely and utterly helpless. Nothing she could do or say helped. Just as the hedgehog I described rejected the milk it was offered, so I rejected all explanations and protestations. After an unbearable two-hour stretch of frozen silence, my friend looked at me and said: 'Joyce! I have needs too.' Don't misunderstand me. She didn't raise her voice. She wasn't angry or aggressive. In fact, she looked helpless and she was choking back tears as she gently whispered this home-truth. This is assertion at its most powerful. It melted my hardness and jolted me out of my self-absorption.

In other words, assertiveness 'believes that, in any given situation, I have needs to be met but so do others. I have rights but others have equal rights. I have a contribution that might be valuable and so do others. The aim of assertion is to ensure that everyone's needs and rights are honoured if at all possible. To be assertive is to love your neighbour as yourself.'[7] Conversely, aggression 'seeks to ignore the rights of others and ignore or dismiss the needs, wants, opinions and feelings of other parties'.[8]

Act swiftly

Jesus encourages us to be assertive.

'This is how I want you to conduct yourself . . . If you enter your place of worship and, about to make an offering, you suddenly remember a grudge a friend has against you, abandon your offering, leave immediately, go to this friend and make things right. Then and only then, come back and work things out with God.
'Or say you're out on the street and an old enemy accosts you. Don't lose a minute. Make the first move; make things right with him.'
(Matt 5:23, 24, *The Message*)

In other words, even though in our view, the fault of the quarrel or the conflict is not ours, it is incumbent on us to make the first move. We have seen how David and Vera Mace modelled this. Both handled anger in themselves and the other less than helpfully. Both went to the other and attempted to work out a solution to the problem.

They also refused to drag their feet. Instead, they dealt with the problem early on in their marriage. Jesus also models to us the importance of keeping short accounts with people. Think, for example, of the events that happened on the night before he died. Peter had sworn allegiance to him. 'Master. I'm ready for anything . . . I'd go to jail for you. I'd *die* for you' (Luke 22:33, *The Message*). In the event, however, he falls asleep in the garden after Jesus had begged him to stay awake and pray. Impulsively and unhelpfully, he slices off a centurion's ear. He runs away when his Master needs moral and spiritual support and to cap it all, he deliberately denies all knowledge of Jesus – not once, but three times. The hurt that these inconsistencies must have inflicted on Jesus are immeasurable. As soon as Jesus emerges from the tomb on that first Easter Day, however, it is evident that he appeared in private to Peter. As the disciples later testified: 'The Lord has risen *and has appeared to Simon*' (Luke 24:34, emphasis mine). What Jesus said or did and how Peter responded are secrets that are locked in their hearts. Although much of this encounter remains enshrouded in mystery, one thing is clear, Jesus did not leave Peter in the agony of his remorse. He initiated the reconciliation process at the first possible opportunity.

Go in weakness – go with a gift

Jesus not only exhorts *us* to go to the one who is separated from us as though by a yawning chasm, he not only models to us the importance of going to that person as soon as possible, he also fleshes out Proverbs 21:14: 'A gift given in secret soothes anger'. Was Peter still angry with himself when he and the other disciples went fishing by the Sea of Galilee that memorable morning John recalls in his Gospel (John 21)? Probably. When we are filled with guilt, we are often filled with self-loathing also and self-loathing is anger turned inwards. Jesus not only attempts to soothe Peter's anger with the surprise, impromptu barbecue on the beach, he gives to Peter an even greater gift – quality time alone with the Master. In taking Peter on one side in the way he did, Jesus took a risk. Peter had already rejected him several times and, in doing so, inflicted not inconsiderable hurt. Instead of protecting himself from further rejection, Jesus lays himself wide open to more injury. Jesus clearly took this risk because his longing for a complete restoration with this disciple he admired and loved was unwavering. Even so, he did not attempt to hasten the process of reconciliation. Rather, he acted cautiously, sensitively, letting Peter set the pace. Instead of making statements, he asked questions: 'Do you truly love me . . .?' And he listened more than he spoke.

Jesus' example suggests that, when we find ourselves in a similar situation to him – when we have been hurt or rejected by someone or when conflict separates us from another, we weigh the options open to us. If we are to take the teaching and example of Jesus seriously, we, too, must go to that person as soon as an appropriate opportunity presents itself. By this I mean that we must choose our time carefully and sensitively so that it is not only convenient for us but a ripe time for the other person also. We will therefore avoid springing a meeting on the other person without explaining why we want to meet with them. We will also avoid occasions when they are already under pressure (like when the vicar or pastor is shaking hands with his congregation at the church door). And we will avoid times when the person concerned is tired or stressed, like when they have just arrived home from work or when they are under pressure from a project – their mind at least half on other things. In other words, we will not only go in love, we will prepare lovingly and prayerfully by thinking creatively and construc- tively. We might consider taking a gift if we can give it in love and if we believe the person can hear its mes- sage without feeling patronised. If we are wise, though, we will go in weakness recognising that we are taking a huge risk; we might well be hurt again. We go pre- pared to take that risk because our longing for recon- ciliation outstrips our fear of being wounded. Because our desire for restoration and unity burns bright, we go prepared to take the process of reconciliation slowly, to ask gentle questions rather than to make dogmatic statements. Like Jesus, we go in love, intent on speak- ing the truth *in love*.

Go humbly

Peter was fortunate, of course. The person seeking rec- onciliation with him was perfect whereas we are far from perfect and will probably approach the reconcil- iatory process with mixed motives. So there are things that we must do which Jesus did not need to do.

We must go humbly, praying that prayer we've already mentioned in this book, the prayer of the pub- lican, 'Lord, have mercy *on me*, a sinner.' In other words, we must go focusing, not so much on the other's faults and misdemeanours so much as on our own. God seemed to underline this lesson for me when I was processing that incident I mentioned earlier in this book – the argument my husband and I had in the mountains when he wanted Coca-Cola and I wanted coffee.

What I wanted to do that day was to give David a piece of my mind: to accuse him of spoiling our day with his selfishness, to punish him by crushing him with my anger. How often so many of us do just this and justify our behaviour by misinterpreting Paul's exhortation that I've just quoted: 'Speak the truth in love' (Eph 4:15). How easily we justify slaughtering another with our anger with reasoning like this: 'I'm tearing him off a strip for his own good. After all, he's got to learn and if I don't teach him, who will?'

By the grace of God, I bridled my tongue that day and crept off, instead, to the spare bedroom that I had turned into a prayer room. There, in pained silence, I took my journal and poured out *to God* the full gamut of my bruised emotions. That day, as I explained in chapter 3, a method of mulling over such incidents was born: *The Seven Es*. I have used and refined it regularly since because it ensures growth and change while preventing wallowing and avoiding stalemate. I recommend it to groups as well as individuals who are would-be reconcilers. It is one way of exercising our God-given ministry of reconciliation. That is why I repeat the exercise here – spelling out the seven steps in greater detail than in chapter 3.

The Seven Es

The first 'E' stands for *event*. It begs us to stand back from the situation and to ask ourselves: 'What was it that triggered off the clash?' By way of response, it can be helpful to jot down a few words or, alternatively, to pour out on paper the whole sad saga as we remember it.

The next 'E' stands for *emotions*. We need to be in touch, not only with the facts but with the feelings also. Significant progress can therefore be made by pausing to respond to another question: 'What emotions has this stirred up in me?' Again, it can be helpful to make a note of words like anger and bitterness, resentment and hatred, disappointment and disillusionment, fear and some of the other words contained in the 'Feelings list' that appears on p 33. Such words take us to the heart of the matter. We become increasingly and acutely aware of the impact the clash has made on ourselves – and self is the only person we can hope to change.

We now need the third 'E' that stands for *evaluate*. We need to evaluate the situation before God by asking ourselves some gentle questions like, 'What am I going to do with these powerful emotions? I could channel the energy they generate into the restoration and upbuilding of the relationship or I could so channel it that the relationship will be further disrupted – even destroyed. At this stage, it can be helpful to re-read Paul's famous ode to love alongside Paul's equally striking definition of 'the old nature', the ego:

> Love is very patient and kind;
> never jealous or envious,
> never boastful or proud,
> never haughty or selfish or rude.
> Love does not demand its own way.
> It is not irritable or touchy.
> It does not hold grudges and will hardly even notice
>   when others do it wrong.
> It is never glad about injustice,
> but rejoices whenever truth wins its way.
> If you love someone you will be loyal . . .
> no matter what the cost.
> You will always believe in him,
> always expect the best of him,
> and always stand your ground in defending him.
>
> (1 Cor 13: 4–7, LB)

> The acts of the sinful nature are obvious: . . . hatred, discord, jealousy, fits of rage, selfish ambition, dissensions, factions and envy . . . and the like.
>
> (Gal 5:19)

At this stage of our reflection, God's Spirit might well convict us that our emotions have ceased to be natural and neutral, instead they have become, or are in danger of becoming, sinful because of the way we are channelling their energy. In this event, before we can make any further progress, we need to confess our own culpability – to lay it at the foot of Christ's cross. We may not be ready to do that yet – especially if we are thrashing around angrily or if bitterness or resentment hold us in their vice-like grip. In fact, it might take days, weeks, even years before we are ready to let go. In that event, we must keep our integrity, tell God we can't or we won't let go and pray, instead, a prayer that goes something like this: 'Help me to be willing to be made willing to let go.' God hears and honours the honesty and integrity of a prayer like that. To him, it is a precious prayer.

We noted earlier in this book that where unresolved conflict exists in potentially powerful relationships, the evil one, the father of lies, is ever active. So our fourth 'E' is *evil one*. In order to become aware of his subversive role in this specific instance it can be productive to ask: 'What is the evil one whispering in my ear about this situation and the people involved?' C.S. Lewis opens our eyes to the accuser's cunning when he puts into the lips of Screwtape, the master demon, this advice:

When two humans have lived together for many years it usually happens that each has tones of voice and expressions of face which are almost unendurably irritating to the other. Work on that. Bring fully into the consciousness of your patient that particular lift of his mother's eyebrows which he learned to dislike in the nursery, and let him think how much he dislikes it. Let him assume that she knows how annoying it is and does it to annoy . . . And, of course, never let him suspect that he has tones and looks which similarly annoy her. As he cannot see or hear himself, this is easily managed.[9]

Yes, Satan persuades us to focus on trivialities: that accent that we can't stand, those mannerisms that irritate us so much or that tone of voice that grates on our over-sensitive ears. With his lying tongue he condemns us, accuses us and mocks us: 'You say you're a Christian and you harbour thoughts like that . . .?' 'If your Christian friends could see you now, what would they say . . .?' Jesus was so skilled in discerning Satan's voice that we can be certain that, if we ask for wisdom and discernment, he will help us to recognise his enemy's involvement and give us the courage and authority to dismiss the evil one and his lies with that authoritative command he, himself, used: 'Away from me, Satan!' (Matt 4:10).

The final three Es provide us with an escape route from the quicksand that threatens to devour our integrity and our very life. The first of the three is *expect*. We can expect God to encounter us – especially if we ask direct questions like, 'Lord, what do you want me to do in this crisis?' We must also pause, of course, as we wait for God to answer. The answer might come through that still, small voice that we have learned to detect, in happier times, is the whisper of God. Alternatively, the answer might come through a passage of Scripture, the advice or questions posed by a friend or a pastor or a counsellor or it might come through one of those 'holy hunches' with which God inspires us from time to time.

The second of the final three life-saving Es is *expose*. Now that we have distinguished between the facts, the feelings and the temptations, we are in a position to expose this untamed jungle to God and to put to him another pressing question: not the one we would like to ask, perhaps, namely: 'When are you going to change _____ so that we can be reconciled?' But rather, a question God seems to enjoy responding to: 'Lord, how do you want *me* to change so that I become more like you and so that _____ and I can be reconciled?'

Even when we can steel ourselves to put such a far-reaching question to God and even when he has answered it, such changes take place painfully slowly. That is why we need the final E which is *exercise patience*. While God re-fashions us and the person with whom there is a rift, if we are to exercise our ministry of reconciliation we may have to wait and wait and wait some more. God, it seems, is rarely in a hurry. We are the ones who insist on having all the i's dotted and the t's crossed, instantly – now.

Those seven Es worked for me that day. They work for me still whenever I seek to work though the Conflict De-escalation Curve opposite.[10]

The diagram reminds me that what I was doing that day was deciding to disengage. Instead of firing the missiles of accusations and insults, blaming and back-biting at David, to call a cease-fire. A cease-fire, claims David Cormack, indicates what we will not do. 'I will not react when I am provoked, I will not take advantage of your unguarded moments; I will not seek your harm and hurt at every – not at any – opportunity.'[11] As well as declaring a cease-fire, David and I together declared a truce – that is, we agreed that the altercation in the mountains had hurt us both, that we would process what had happened, first on our own, then together. When we came together, we would talk about it, re-run it to see how different it could have been and, hopefully, grow from the experience. We recognised and acknowledged that we did not want conflict of this nature to continue, we both wanted to change and be changed. In other words, we resolved voluntarily to abandon our entrenched positions – which is what the word 'withdrawal' means in the diagram.

In retrospect, I recognise how vital this withdrawal is. As we saw in chapter 7, whether we respond to disagreements by competing or withdrawing, by compromising or giving in, we are all aiming for the same thing: to control or manipulate the relationship by our

Conflict Escalation and De-Escalation Curve

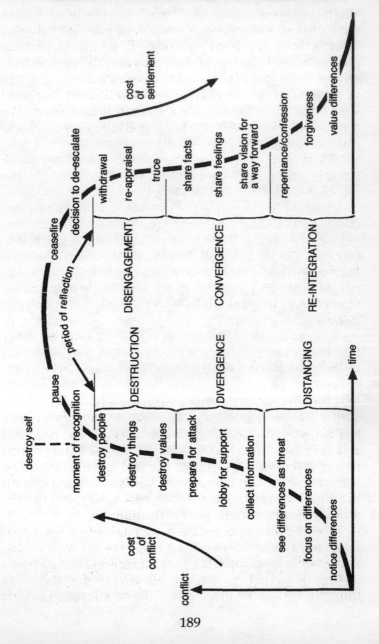

189

response. When we withdraw, however, we make a non-verbal commitment to attempt to cease from keeping a firm hand on the controls and to seek unity instead. By unity I mean that blending of insights and life-styles that frees us to relinquish our selfish demand that life must be lived my way.

This step is so costly that it is, perhaps, little wonder that it rarely happens – or, if it happens at all, it doesn't last. I think, for example, of Jesus himself. W.H. Vanstone suggests that the main reason why Jesus sweated blood in the garden of Gethsemane was not because he feared the nails, nor that he shunned the shame, nor even because he recoiled from the seeming abandonment of his Father. The reason why the sorrow almost crushed him to death was because the moment had come when he must relinquish the reins of his life and hand them over to his enemies. When he left Gethsemane, he no longer masterminded events as he had done up to this point in the drama. When he left Gethsemane he had abdicated control. Others took charge.

Jesus' relinquishing control, however, did not spell impotence. As we have already noted, he achieved more in the three days that followed his superhuman sacrifice of his own will than he had achieved in the previous thirty years of his life. Curiously, the same applies to us. When we exchange independence for inter-dependence, we, too, achieve more for God, the Kingdom and our relationships than we ever did when we insisted on going it alone.

Stage 1, the Disengagement Phase, is, however, in very many ways, the easiest and least costly part of reconciliation. The others are more demanding which is why the model might helpfully be called a De-escalation Climb rather than a De-escalation Curve. The word 'curve' makes the process seem so simple. It is far from simple. That is why we go on to devote a whole chapter each to two of the steps involved: sharing and forgiving. Before rushing on to another chapter, though, I recommend that we pause to reflect – using some of the following exercises to give God time and space to show us where we are succeeding and where we still need to grow.

Suggested exercises

1. Re-read the peace prayer attributed to Francis of Assisi on p 175. Read it slowly and prayerfully. If you come to a word or phrase or sentence that you can't pray with integrity, stop. Ask yourself, 'What memories have been triggered that have prevented me from praying this prayer?' If the memories don't come on their own, ask God to remind you of them.

2. Re-read the definitions of assertion and aggression on p 179. Then read the two letters that follow. They were printed in a certain magazine shortly after that magazine had appeared with a front-page photograph of Mother Teresa of Calcutta:

Letter 1:
'My wife and I have just returned from three months of living and working in Cairo, Egypt. I was over there as a volunteer with the International Executive Service Corps . . . While in Egypt, my wife, Pat, volunteered her services in three areas of need . . . Four days a week she worked in two of four missions serving under Mother Teresa's name. What a blessed experience that was! They too are incarnate examples of "walking humbly".
'The sisters mostly care for baby girls who have literally been trashed nearby in the city dump. Most of them are terribly afflicted with birth defects of every description. It is an authentic rescue mission! The love and care that they receive is incredible – all God!'

Letter 2:

'Please remove us from your mailing list . . . The last straw was when you had Sister Teresa on your cover!

'She believes, from what I've read, that no matter what religion we are – Buddhist, Hindu, Catholic, etc – we all come to Jesus in the end. Jesus clearly states that "*no* man comes to the Father but by Me!" Her doctrine is clearly unscriptural and we want no part of it . . .

Doing good deeds like Sister Teresa (I won't call her Mother), won't get anyone into heaven. To have poems written about how she exemplifies the Christian life is wrong in my book. Christianity is a relationship not a lifestyle. We all know Catholicism is steeped in idolatry. Why put her up as a model . . . '12

What emotions came to the surface in you as you read the aggressive letter? Do you know why? How do you want to channel these emotions?

3. Re-read the version of 1 Corinthians 13:4–7 that is quoted on p 73. Think of occasions when you have attempted to sort out a conflict situation with someone. Think back over your actions and your attitudes. Place them alongside the plumb-line of this passage and ask yourself, 'Did I go in love?' If not, what were you trying to achieve? Do you owe anyone an apology?

4. If there is a rift between you and someone else at the moment, take another look at the seven Es. Apply them to the situation you are currently working through. See if they help.

5. Take a careful look at the Contract for Dealing With Unresolved Conflict that follows. Think of the

people you are close to or the groups you belong to. Could you make this sort of commitment with these relationships in mind? If not, why not? What would you want to change:

A Contract
for Dealing With Unresolved Conflict

A contract is an agreement between two people who love each other and want to work towards building a better relationship. It is best made at a time when neither person is feeling hurt or angry.

Step 1 I own my anger

I acknowledge that my anger is mine and that no one can *make* me angry. It is therefore never true to say, 'You make me angry'. This accusation might produce a defensive reaction in you and thus widen the cleavage that separates us.

So I refuse to believe that you make me angry or that your action is responsible for my pain or even that you are responsible for making me feel better. I even let go of the demand that you must change in the way I prescribe. Instead, I will try to come to terms with the realisation that, when I am angry, heated emotion flares up from somewhere deep within *me*. I am responsible both for the feeling and for the way I choose to process and to channel it. Instead of demanding that you change until you become the person *I* want you to be, I will share with you *in love* how I perceive and feel about you and how I perceive and feel about the differences that divide us. I will explore with you ways of ensuring that clashes and disagreements draw us closer to one another rather than prising us apart from one another.

Step 2 I will tell you when I am angry

I promise to share my anger with you as soon as I am

aware of it or at a time as soon afterwards as seems appropriate. I recognise that it can be helpful to have a cooling off period before saying anything so I will not be in a hurry to spell out the anger and the cause of it. Instead I will learn to contain my anger without repressing it.

I will always attempt to speak the truth *in love.*

I will recognise that it can sometimes be helpful to work the anger out of my system in a physical way: by going out for a run, playing badminton, doing the iron-ing, chopping wood, punching a pillow. I will recog-nise that, though this defuses the problem it does not solve it. I will therefore recognise the value of learning to process my anger.

Step 3 I will not hammer you with my anger
When I am angry, I will not attack you physically or verbally.

I will not bring up old issues – reciting a well-rehearsed record of the wrongs you have done.

I will not choose an inappropriate time to tell you that I am angry – like when you are hungry or tired

I will try not to have a temper tantrum or let my emo-tions control the situation

I will not blame or accuse you.

I will refrain from using catch phrases like: 'You always . . . ', 'You never . . .'

I will not leave God out of the conflict but will sur-round the whole situation with prayer.

Step 4 I promise to ask you to help me with my anger

In order to do this, when I am angry or have been angry, I will say to you:

'When you ....I become angry. Will you please help me?'

Step 5 I will attempt to support you when you are angry

When you are angry, I will try to:

Listen to you – not simply to the words you say but to the underlying feelings.

Accept you and acknowledge your right to feel angry. I will neither judge you nor demand that you explain the situation to me in full unless you choose to.

Validate you – let you know that it is all right for you to be angry even though I may not fully understand why a certain situation infuriated you.

Understand you – I may not fully understand but I will try. I will attempt to see how the situation looks from your point of view. I want you to know that I care about you and I really want to understand things as you see them.

Step 6 I will try to avoid using conversation stoppers:

I will try to avoid:

Shutting you up by saying or implying: 'You shouldn't feel that way.'

Trivialising by saying,' There, there, you'll be all right.'

Blaming by saying 'You have no right to be angry.'

Step 7: I will express the full gamut of my emotions (hatred, bitterness, resentment) **to God** rather than to you.

Step 8: I will hand over the anger to God and let him sift it

Step 9 I will exercise patience while God transforms you and me

Step 10 I will ask: 'Lord, how do you want *me* to change so that our relationship can be more harmonious?

I recognise that I may break this contract. Whenever this happens, I will re-read it and try to understand and learn from the reasons why I broke it.[13]

6. Study the Conflict Escalation and De-escalation Curve so that its stages are familiar to you before you read on.

9

SPEAKING THE TRUTH IN LOVE

The least costly part of the painful process of reconciliation is stage one: calling a ceasefire, declaring a truce, unhooking ourselves from those with whom we have been locked in conflict. That's what we observed in the last chapter. The most costly part is stage two: the convergence phase. Even when the situation becomes so unbearable that something or someone clearly has to give, convergence poses problems.

When we understand what is involved in the convergence phase, it is not difficult to see why many people opt out at this point. According to David Cormack, 'convergence is a process of coming together, of understanding . . . of sharing'.[1]

Coming together with people you've been at variance with; people who have hurt or insulted or grated on or offended you? *Understanding* people whose behaviour patterns or personality or attitudes are so radically different from your own? *Sharing*, that is intimately exchanging not only facts but *feelings*[2] with someone you've been at loggerheads with or with someone you dislike intensely simply for who they are? The very thought produces fear, even panic in some. Distance seems so much safer and more sensible than closeness.

Yet creating appropriate closeness is vital because, when people clash, they not only recoil from one another, hostility keeps them from communicating as we observed in earlier chapters. In diagrammatic terms, the sequence of events goes something like this:

Harmony

Clash-point   **Freeze**

A Gulf

Here we have two (or more) people creating a harmonious relationship. Conflict erupts or, for some reason, call it 'chemistry', they grate on one another's nerves, and one of two things happen. Either over-heated emotions boil over and a violent clash ensues or the intensity of their feelings becomes so strong that they are pushed into an emotional deep-freeze and the result is a cold war. In either eventuality, the people recoil from one another – bemused, even frightened – and become separated by a gulf.

The gulf is natural, neutral and necessary at this stage. It provides everyone concerned with an opportunity to face reality – that the relationship is under serious threat. It also gives everyone time and space to process that internal struggle we face when powerful feelings like anger and hurt, hatred and resentment, the desire and determination to accuse, blame and retaliate mingle with, at best, the yearning for reconciliation, growth and peace and, at worst, the guilt that goads: 'You ought to want to be reconciled'. In other words, the gulf brings the people who are clashing to make-or-break point. They now have at least two options: to face the challenge of discussing the differences that are driving them to turn their backs on one another rather than to face one another or so to focus on and magnify the differences that the escalation of the conflict relentlessly pursues the course illustrated in the Escalation Curve on p 121.

Conflict-avoiders, conflict-deniers and certain conflict-enjoyers often run away from the painful process of placing all the cards on the table by communicating in this open manner. Consequently, the gulf between them is not only perpetuated, it widens:

The Gulf Widens

Coldness, mistrust and suspicion then creep into and take hold of the relationship. The people concerned may glance over their shoulders at one another from time to time. They may even talk to others about their 'enemy'. The aim of any such dialogue, however, is often sick as the Escalation Curve shows. Because differences are now perceived as personal threats, its purpose is to gather ammunition in preparation for an attack, to bolster the already jaundiced view of the opponent, to lobby for support in the impending all-out-fight for supremacy. In determining to do battle rather than to seek to understand and be understood, the perpetrators of the destruction phase frequently feast on tittle-tattle – those tasty morsels of gossip on which, according to the writer of Proverbs, our hearts delight to feed (Prov 18:8).

Before the participants in such unresolved conflict situations can become reconciled, then, the wheels of two-way communication (sharing and sensitive listening) need to be restored. 'That means spending time together talking: sharing where we are, what we did in the conflict and why, how we saw the other party and how we interpreted his action.'[3] Convergence not only involves sharing such facts. Convergence 'must also bring the parties together emotionally and spiritually'.[4]

The last part, establishing or re-establishing emotional and spiritual oneness, is the most difficult for several reasons. One is that many people are embarrassed to share feelings because they do not have a vocabulary for airing the emotions with which they are riddled when they are caught in the crossfire of conflict: feelings of fear, maybe, or loneliness, anger, isolation, restlessness, bitterness, hatred – the list seems endless. Another reason is that when we embark on an intimate sharing of *feelings* as well as facts, we make ourselves vulnerable. When we divulge *feelings*, we take a series of huge risks – the risk of being misunderstood, or, worse, of being rejected: of having someone reprimand us with a cutting comment like: 'You shouldn't feel like that'; the risk of being crushed by unkindness, cruelty or insensitivity; the risk, not only of being disliked but of being dismissed by a comment, a look or an attitude. Before we dare embark on the path that leads to establishing emotional and spiritual oneness, indeed, before we can even contemplate coming to the negotiation table, we may need to seek to understand the complexity of communication skills.

Transmitting messages

By communication skills I mean the twin arts of transmitting messages accurately and sensitively and of listening to others conveying the truth as they perceive it.

Although such two-way communication may sound like child's play, as natural as blinking, experience warns us that sending and receiving messages is far more hazardous than it seems. One reason that has come to light in recent years is that, as the Communication Components' Diagram reveals, 'seven out of ten of the components in communication have nothing to do with speech.'[5]

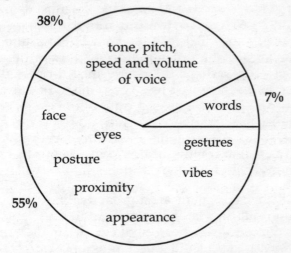

Communication Components Diagram

In other words, communication is a complex, multi-faceted craft that needs to be learned and practised and that can always be improved. This is humbling for some. A mystery for others. 'Why,' they ask, 'has no one ever told us that when we try to transmit a message, words play such a comparatively insignificant role? Why has no one ever explained that, while words communicate a mere 7% of the message, the tone and volume of the voice, the silences and pauses, tears and sighs, the pitch and speed of the speech transmit a massive 38%?' 'Why has no one opened our eyes to the fact that our facial expression, gestures, bodily posture, eye contact and appearance contribute 55% of the message we are attempting to convey?'

Such people find it enlightening to discover why eye contact, for example is so powerful. David Cormack puts it persuasively:

The eyes are the windows of our souls. In our eyes, for those who can read them, are messages which drown our words and outshine the most dazzling of smiles. We can control our mouth, but our pupils contract and dilate without our bidding and signal our appreciation or rejection of those around. Eye contact is perhaps the single most important non-verbal message we give. Too often, our warm smile stops at our mouths and our cold eyes tell the real message. What does your face do for your communications? Does it reinforce them or betray them? If you want to communicate – look at your listeners. If you want to hear, look at the speaker![6]

Equally, we communicate a great deal about ourselves through our smiles and frowns, our grins and grimaces, our gestures, head shakes and nods. And our emotions make use of our hands and our bodies to make their presence felt and understood.

As I have explained in detail in *Listening to Others*,[7] years ago, a man crippled with arthritis used to come regularly to me for help. As he spilled out his worries, he would mutilate the spider plant that sat on the table next to the settee where he normally sat. Or he would take a paper tissue from his pocket and tug at it nervously or angrily, tearing it to shreds. As I watched him, I realised just how accurately his hands were picking up and expressing his feelings. In fact, his hands, his pain-racked body and his eyes gave me far more insight into his situation than the meagre words he managed to stammer.

The way he dressed also used to alert me to the way

he was feeling on any given occasion. Addressing teams, David Cormack invites them to 'think for a moment about the silent signals that you give each time your team meets. How do you dress for the team meeting – formally or informally? – neatly or untidily? Will the other members recognise that meeting with them is important to you by the way you have prepared yourself?'[8]

Eyes, bodily posture, gestures, facial expression, appearance, all contribute to the message we are attempting to convey. So does the tone and volume of our voice together with the speed and pitch of our speech and the silences and tears with which our words may well be punctuated. Take silences, for example. There are all kinds of reasons why we might pause when we are trying to convey a message that really matters to us. We might be worried, and anxiety has a habit of slowing down our ability to think clearly. Or we might be the kind of person who reflects before they say anything. We will therefore need to pause frequently as we fumble for words that accurately express our feelings. Or embarrassment might so paralyse us that we pause because pain prevents us from speaking.

I think, for example, of someone who once came to share a problem with me. After we had talked about nothing in particular for a while, apologetically she stuttered: 'I'm sorry. I'm not sure I'm going to be able to tell you why I've come.' I invited her to take her time and only to speak when she felt ready whereupon we sat in silence for a full fifteen minutes. Finally, she whispered, 'Maybe, if you could give me paper and pencil, I could write the word down?' I fetched paper and pencil and prayed as she wrote one solitary word: INCEST. Tears filled her eyes as she handed the paper back to me. Like silence, tears are a language. Although she had uttered the minimum of words, she had conveyed a profound, pain-filled but powerful message.[9]

Receiving messages

The message may well have fallen onto deaf ears, however, if she had shared with someone who was waiting for a stream of words. That is why the need is not simply to discover how to *share* meaningfully, in addition, we need to learn to listen sensitively and attentively. Indeed, we dare not claim that effective communication has taken place until this happens:

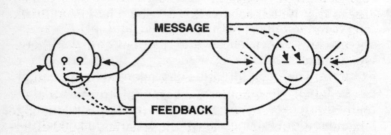

Two-way Communication[10]

The reason why I make this claim is that, when the person sharing says his or her piece, communication has only just begun. The process is not completed until the person listening reflects back in some way what he or she has heard, seen and detected. The reason why this active listening is paramount is that, whenever we listen to anyone, we receive what they are saying through the filter of our own presuppositions and prejudices, hopes and fears, expectations and dreads, culture and conditioning to mention just a few of the factors involved. In other words, there is a sense in which our ability to receive messages accurately is severely limited, if not impaired. We are selective listeners, hearing what we want to hear. As John and Agnes Sturt remind us, 'Ultimately, I cannot tell you what you have said, I can only tell you what I think I have heard.'[11]

For this reason, active listening entails clarifying so

that we ensure that the message we are hearing is the same message the speaker intended to convey. When my arthritic friend used to settle on my settee and sigh, saying: 'I've been bad this week,' for example, I needed to clarify what he meant by this rather nebulous shorthand he frequently used. Sometimes the complaint meant that he was in considerable pain in which case the way he walked from the front door to the lounge would have given me a clue. On other occasions, though, he would use exactly the same words to mean that he felt ashamed because he had been drinking heavily. On yet other occasions, he would be trying to tell me that he despaired of ever finding employment.

Vague words like 'bad' are not the only ones that are ambiguous. Communication experts inform us that the five hundred most used words in the English language 'have, according to standard dictionaries, 14,000 different definitions'.[12] Some of these words have more than one hundred meanings each. Unless we clarify that the definition that springs to our mind as we listen is the same definition that the person we are listening to is applying, we could easily find that mis-communication rather than accurate communication is taking place.

Listening with our eyes and senses

As we have already noted in this chapter, however, the bulk of a message is transmitted non-verbally. In fact, it is estimated that we receive more than 75% of a message through our eyes:

76% through sight
12% from hearing
6% through touch
3% from smell
3% from taste.

'Watch how two people enter a house,' invites Anne Long in *Listening*:

Laura comes through the front door with her head down, apart from a quick anxious glimpse at me, her inert body creeping rather than walking up the stairs and she doesn't utter a word. Gina enters head up, open-faced with a warm smile, stretching out both arms in greeting and chattering all the way up the stairs. Our bodies often describe our spirits – the slumped or upright shoulders, the hands that are relaxed or that pluck nervously at a sleeve, the body that flings itself in abandonment into a chair or sits tensely on the edge.[13]

Yes. We need to train our eyes to become good 'listeners'. As well as listening with our ears and our eyes, we also need to learn to listen with our senses – to pick up what Michael Jacobs calls 'the bass line' that undergirds the melody of the main message. In communication terms this means that we tune in, not only to the words we hear, the eyes and body language that we read but to those unexpressed emotions that throb through the message with the persistence of a recurring and insistent drum-beat. Or, to change the metaphor, we need to become sensitive to 'the vibes'.

David Cormack alerts us to yet another lesson we must learn – the language of proximity – of space and distance. As he, himself, explains:

Physical proximity – how close you stand to people – carries with it messages of trust or suspicion. Social distance is the space that people prefer to keep around them. With strangers, as in a lift, it is surprisingly large. Given the opportunity, most people stand two or three feet from you – normally on the opposite side of the lift! . . . Acquaintances stand closer, and friends are touching . . . The Teach Yourself book on non-verbal behaviour shows that the areas we allow friends and relatives to touch vary according to the nature of the relationship.

Physical contact is a powerful reinforcer of words. If you want to show pleasure, concern, affection, trust . . . these may all be conveyed by touch. No words need be spoken, but in addition to words, physical contact creates a communication not readily forgotten.[14]

We do well, then, to observe whether a person creates distance because they are, perhaps anxious or suspicious or whether they come close because, perhaps, they feel safe or trusting.

Listening in this way with our senses and our eyes is fraught with difficulties, however. Just as it is easy to misunderstand a *word* a speaker uses, so it is even more possible to misinterpret the language of someone's eyes or face or body or space. It is therefore imperative that, instead of *assuming* that we have heard correctly, we clarify. As John and Agnes Sturt remind us, assume can be spelt ASS-U-ME. In other words, if you *assume* that you have understood my message, you might make an ass out of you and me!

We may chuckle at that reminder, but the results of assuming are far-reaching and painful. As I write, I have in front of me a copy of a letter that I once wrote to someone whose comments to me had seemed cruel and cutting at a time when I felt peculiarly vulnerable. In the letter, I refer, not only to what I heard the person say but to the message I received through his eyes and body-language. With the wisdom of hindsight, I can clearly see how my letter compounded the problem. Instead of asking whether my interpretation was accurate, I assumed that what I saw was what he had intended to communicate. I did, indeed, make an ass of myself on that occasion. Such sad, damaging incidents convince me that improving and practising communication skills is the task of a lifetime. Unless we continually learn and practise and improve, we will never succeed in doing what Paul begs the Ephesians to do:

'Make every effort to keep the unity of the Spirit through the bond of peace . . . [and speak] the truth in love' (Eph 4:3, 15).

It is easier to speak rather glibly about 'speaking the truth in love' than to learn this form of communication for which David Augsburger has coined a word: 'care-fronting'. Care-fronting is so crucial to reconciliation that I propose to examine its components in some detail.

Care-fronting, as the word implies, is a mixture of caring and confronting. By caring, I mean the genuine longing to promote another's well-being coupled with the ability to communicate concern and unconditional love. As David Augsburger puts it, 'The core of true caring is a clear invitation to grow, to become what he or she is and can be, to move toward maturity . . . [to] set another free . . . Caring requires that one get interested in the direction the other's life is taking and offer real immediate involvement. If you love, you level. If you value another, you volunteer the truth.'[15]

It follows that caring is a pre-requisite for true reconciliation. We cannot make peace unless we care.

By confrontation, I do not mean the kind of cold, calculated, cruel criticism that insists: 'I'm jolly well going to give so and so a piece of my mind – someone has to do it.' That is aggression not genuine confrontation. Neither am I using the word to mean a verbal ding-dong. That, too, is aggressive rather than confrontational behaviour. I am using the word 'confrontation' in the way Michael Jacobs defines it when he writes, 'Confrontation is not a means of trying to catch a person out, of making him appear small, or of punishing him . . . neither is it the iron fist in the velvet glove, but rather the "still small voice" which speaks more clearly than the earthquake, wind and fire.'[16] Confrontation is the courage and ability gently and clearly to express a point of view that may differ from and even challenge the viewpoint or behaviour of another. Confrontation is the peaceful process by which we pinpoint and clarify differences that have been contributing to the clash that drove us apart from someone *so that* we may move on to establish the threads (however thin they might seem) that potentially bind us together in respect and mutual care. It follows that confrontation of this kind is also a pre-requisite for true reconciliation.

The challenge that the call to speak the truth in love presents us with is the challenge to care-front during the convergence phase. Instead of doing this automatically, our thinking, if we were to stop to analyse it, runs along lines like these:

> If I want to show genuine care, I dare not confront. Confronting would seem like a contradiction of caring. And if I want to confront, I must not muddy the waters by expressing care. Caring would weaken the confrontation. If I am to confront effectively, I must leave caring on one side for the time being. If, on the other hand, I am to care genuinely, honest, open confrontation must be sacrificed.[17]

Such assumptions incite a persuasive protest from David Augsburger. True caring, and true confrontation can be expressed at one and the same time. Care-fronting communicates 'with both impact and respect, with truth and love.'[18] Care-fronting is the way to 'speak the truth in love'.

Taking Jesus as our model

Jesus exercised the gift of care-fronting so memorably that we cannot do better than take him as our model.

Think, for example, of a scenario John presents us with. Jesus is sitting in the Temple teaching the people who have swarmed around him. He looks up to see an undignified group of Pharisees and religious scholars dragging behind them a woman who has been caught committing adultery. Pushing her forward in full view of the crowd, the religious leaders try to trap and incriminate Jesus by asking him a trick question:

'Teacher, this woman was caught red-handed in the act of adultery. Moses, in the Law, gives orders to stone such persons. What do you say?'

Jesus could have retorted aggressively: 'It takes two to commit adultery. Where is the man involved?' He could have added, equally aggressively, 'You quote the Law. As you know, the Law requires that two witnesses who have *seen* the crime must give evidence before a person can be condemned. Compromising circumstances are not enough.' He could have used sarcasm: 'So you believe in misquoting the Law do you? As you well know, the punishment you refer to applies only if the woman referred to is a betrothed virgin. In that event the Law requires the execution of *both* parties – not just the woman (Deut 22:23, 24)'. Instead, he pauses. Why does he bend down in the way John describes? Why does he write in the dust with his finger? What does he write? Could it be that he is processing his own emotions, sending an arrow prayer to his Father, seizing the opportunity, however brief, to clarify his thinking? Could it be that, on the one hand, he is burning with compassion for the woman while, on the other hand, blazing with anger at the hypocrisy of the religious leaders? Or could it be that he is consumed with compassion for both the woman *and* her misguided oppressors?

Sadly, we lack certain clues that would help us to interpret his response accurately. If only we could see his face as he speaks. If only we could look into his eyes. If only we could hear the tone and the pitch and the pace of his voice as he simply says: 'If any one of you is without sin, let him be the first to throw a stone at her' (John 8:7).

Why does he move his gaze again from the faces of the woman's accusers to the ground? Could it be that it is out of compassion for those who are about to lose face – those who keep their integrity at last by abandoning the woman to the mercy of Jesus? Could it be that his downcast eyes are filled with sadness? Could it be that what we are witnessing is an expression of carefronting? Possibly, for Jesus longs for the salvation of the Pharisees and religious scholars just as much as he longs that people like this female victim of male dominance should be rescued. He confronts because he cares, not because he is enraged.

He now turns to the woman. Picture him straightening up and looking at her forlorn face and bedraggled body. Listen as he addresses her – using that same word he will use to address his mother when she stands gazing at him hanging on the cross – that gentle word that is laced with unprecedented respect: 'Woman'. Imagine the scene and the tone of voice as he asks her: 'Has no one condemned you?' Hear her hesitant, incredulous, respectful response: 'No one, sir.' Observe Jesus' care-fronting technique. Does he smile as he proclaims his own astonishing, undeserved verdict: 'Neither do I condemn you'? Does he stretch out his hand to touch her reassuringly as he admonishes her: 'Go now and leave your life of sin' (John 8:11)?

Ponder Jesus' words, 'Neither do I condemn you . . . Go now and leave your life of sin.' In those two pithy statements we witness the skill and the kindness with which Jesus wove together both caring and confronting. The woman surely would never forget that day – and neither would the crowd. It was as though Jesus' own parable of the Prodigal Son was being enacted before their very eyes.

Did the crowd realise that day that, although Jesus was both caring for and confronting the woman and the religious leaders, what he did *not* say spoke volumes. He did not say to the woman, 'Go now and leave your life of sin but remember, if you sin again, I won't be there to support you. Instead, I'll join your accusers.'

No. He simply said, 'Go now and leave your life of sin.' Even if she continues to live promiscuously, his love for her will not dwindle, it will continue. As we serve our apprenticeship in learning the art of care-fronting, we, too must remember that 'confrontation invites another to change but does not demand it. The con-fronter does not make the continuation of the friend-ship hang on a change of life in the confrontee . . . Acceptance does not exclude differing; it frees us to dif-fer more fully, frankly, effectively.'[19] The care-confron-ter believes and enacts the following:

'I differ from you.
> (To differ is not to reject.)
I disagree with you.
> (To disagree is not to attack.)
I will confront you.
> (To confront is to complement.)
I will invite change.
> (To change is to grow.)[20]

Paving the way

If we are to communicate in the demanding, two-pronged manner we have sketched in this chapter, we need to prepare to encounter those with whom we are incompatible carefully and sensitively. First, then, we need to earmark a mutually convenient and acceptable time when we can sit down with the person or persons with whom we have clashed with the express purpose of sharing in the way that I have described. Such time-fixing is as essential for close friends or spouses as it is for members of a team or acquaintances. Of itself, it conveys a powerful message: 'Our relationship is so important to me that I want to give it one of the most precious gifts I have – my time.'

As well as arranging a time, we need to give careful thought to the place where we will meet. A venue that is as congenial as possible to all parties concerned will best provide the atmosphere needed for the desired convergence. And, of course, it will be vital that privacy can be guaranteed and the likelihood of interruptions minimised. For this reason, if at all possible, the telephone should be unplugged and individuals should agree to switch off their mobile phones if they have them.

A time and a place, however convenient and congenial, are of little use unless we have planned a procedure. Two possible procedures present themselves: discussion, or writing followed by discussion.

Let's look at writing followed by discussion first. By this I mean that a group or two people who are recovering from the aftermath of a clash come together with two aims in mind: one, to pin-point what went wrong and two, to discover a way forward. In order to find the longed-for way forward, instead of relying only on the spoken word, opportunity is given to each person present to take part in the jigsaw puzzle approach. By this I mean that each person present recognises that they and each of the others have unique hopes and needs, rights and expectations that must be heeded and heard. Opportunity is therefore provided for each person to define the problem or sum up the issue under discussion as they perceive it and also to express, in writing, their expectations and the reasons why they cherish them. To facilitate this process a handout will have been prepared which might look like 'The Jigsaw' on the following page.

First, individuals fill in their names which means that they are identifiable and will write only those things that they are happy others should read. Next, they list any hopes, expectations and perceived needs that seem relevant to the task in hand. They then record the reasons why they want and expect these particular things from this particular person or Are they, for example, born of basic beliefs, current emotional or

The Jigsaw

Defining the Problem:

Person...

Problem: As I see it, the problem/issue is:

....
....
....
....
....
....
....
....
....

My expectations are

....
....
....
....
....
....
....
....
....
....

Reasons

....
....
....
....
....
....
....
....
....[21]

physical or spiritual needs – or are there other reasons? When the persons concerned have had ample time to reflect on and respond to the questions concerned, quality time must be given to examining each piece of the puzzle. This may be achieved by spreading the pieces of the 'jigsaw' on a table or on the floor and giving everyone ample opportunity to read and reflect on the responses each person has made.

Bearing in mind what has been highlighted about communication in this chapter, opportunity should also be given to each person to explain verbally what they intended to say. If this is to prove a healing rather than a hurting experience, it will be important that members of the group or twosome agree beforehand that each person's expectations and needs are valid even though they may not be fully accepted or understood by each of the other persons concerned.

Having heard and validated each person's point of view, opportunity should then be given for clarification so that the group is as certain as it can be that the messages being transmitted are being accurately received. In addition, it may be necessary to pursue some or all of the following questions:

- Why is this desire being expressed at this moment in time?
- What would it mean to you if your expectations were realised?
- Are there any alternatives that would achieve the same goal?
- How might you feel if your proposals and hopes prove impractical or impossible?
- What might happen if your hopes were dashed and your expectations laid on one side for the sake of the group?
- What is your worst fear?
- Under what circumstances would you be prepared to abandon this particular hope for the sake of the

group or the relationship?
- Be specific. What, precisely, do you want to happen? What would assure you that it is happening?

The next task is to discover where the needs and hopes and expectations and fears being expressed dovetail and from this to discern the values, the ideals and the vision that the people concerned share. At the same time, care and time must be given to ensure that complex areas that need further attention and creative exploration are not ignored but explored. It follows that one meeting may well prove to be insufficient – that subsequent occasions should be arranged so that each person in the group feels understood and heard, valued and needed. It follows, too, that the services of a facilitator might become necessary. Such a facilitator would need to be someone who has earned the respect of each member of the group or twosome, someone who can be objective as they piece together the information that has been shared and someone who is genuinely in a position to care-front.

The reason for suggesting that people pave the way for verbal sharing by responding to the handout above (or something similar) is that such a questionnaire offers each person concerned an equal opportunity to voice their opinion. A piece of paper doesn't cry or look intimidating or scowl or interrupt. Pieces of paper wait patiently while each person searches for the words they need to convey their message. And the questionnaire enables each person to see clearly, not only their own points of view but the perceptions and viewpoints of others. In other words, it provides a structure for dialogue, a forum for each person to open up, an opportunity where the truth may be spelt out in love and ways forward explored.

Letter writing
When only two people are involved, say a husband

and wife or two close friends, while the above exercise might still prove more than worthwhile, another written exercise presents itself. This piece of written work also begins by both parties identifying precisely what the problem or the issue is – like the question of appearance, for example. They then turn the topic into a 'feelings' question since the aim of the exercise is primarily to establish *feelings* rather than facts. In other words, they agree to write a letter to one another taking as their topic the question: How do I feel about the way you dress? They write amicably but honestly for some ten minutes, then they exchange letters and read what the other has written before discussing the contents of both letters.

While learning the difficult art of transmitting and receiving messages, many married couples, including ourselves, have been indebted to this exercise for clarifying problems and for growing in our understanding of the person to whom we have committed ourselves in love.

Re-running a quarrel

Some couples value yet another variation on this theme. When they have quarrelled for some reason, in order that convergence might take place, they agree on a place and a time when they might meet to discuss a particular problem and they agree to 're-run' the quarrel. In other words, they agree to think back over the clash and, being careful to avoid communication blocks like blaming or accusing, they write to each other suggesting ways in which each might have acted and reacted differently. They then exchange letters and discuss the suggestions made bearing in mind that the object of the exercise is to discover ways in which they might foster the growth of their relationship and set one another free to become the people God created them to be.

The exercises I have mentioned provide a framework in which we may speak the truth in love. If the exercises are to succeed, we do well to bear in mind that:

A context of caring must come before confrontation.
A sense of support must be present before criticism
A basis of trust must be laid before one risks advising.
A floor of affirmation must undergird any assertive-
- ness.
A gift of understanding opens the way to disagreeing.
An awareness of love sets us free to level with each other.[22]

Further exercises

1. Learn the above powerful quotation off by heart and seek to put it into practice.

2. If you and a friend or a spouse or a colleague or member of the family misinterpret what one another has said, instead of having an argument, suggest the, 'Let's play it again' exercise I mentioned in chapter six. Re-run the conversation in such a way that all possible misunderstandings are ironed out.

3. Assess your own ability to care-front, to speak the truth in love, by thinking of an occasion when you have challenged someone. Ask yourself the following questions to establish whether you genuinely spoke the truth in love or whether you merely ventilated your own hurt feelings, anger or frustration:

• Did I genuinely *care-front*? That is, did I confront only after experiencing genuine *care* for the person and as an expression of real concern for them?
• Was my care-fronting *gentle*? Or was my tone of voice harsh, my eyes steely, my attitude judgmental, my intention to apportion blame, to accuse or

even to threaten?
- Was my care-fronting *constructive*? That is, did I open windows through which the person(s) could peep and see concrete ways in which they could change and become more Christlike and mature?
- Did I care-front *acceptably*? Did I take into consideration any possible misinterpretations the person(s) could have placed on what I said? Did I use criticism? If so, why? What does that tell me about my level of caring?
- Was my care-fronting *clear*? That is, did I separate my feelings from the facts and both feelings and facts from my own interpretation of the situation? Or did I fall into the trap of expressing my interpretation as though it was a fact? Was my care-fronting offered at an appropriate time and in a congenial place for the listener? If not, what might it have communicated – did it, in fact, sound less than caring or counter-productive because it raised the already-mounting stress level in the listener?
- Did I abdicate by turning my back on an opportunity to care-front? If so, why?[24]

4. Respond to the questionnaire on the next page that asks: Are You a Good Listener?

5. Think back over the past week and try to recall when and where you have been touched. Ask yourself what that touch conveyed to you. Ask yourself, too, when and where you have touched others and what you were attempting to communicate by physical contact. Then set yourself the task of observing those who touch you in the coming week – as well as those who keep their distance. Notice how you feel about their actions and reactions. If necessary, refer to the list of feelings at the end of chapter one to help you pinpoint precisely what your reactions are.

Are You a Good Listener?

ATTITUDES	Almost Always	Occasionally		Almost Never
1. Do you like to listen to other people talk?	5	4	3	2	1
2. Do you encourage other people to talk?	5	4	3	2	1
3. Do you listen, even if you do not like the person who is talking?	5	4	3	2	1
4. Do you listen equally well whether the person talking is man or woman, young or old, black or white?	5	4	3	2	1
5. Do you listen equally well to friend, acquaintance and stranger?	5	4	3	2	1

ACTIONS

When talking to, or listening to someone –

6. Do you put what you have been doing out of sight and out of mind?	5	4	3	2	1
7. Do you look at the speaker?	5	4	3	2	1
8. Do you try to ignore the distractions about you?	5	4	3	2	1
9. Do you smile, nod your head, and otherwise encourage the speaker to talk?	5	4	3	2	1
10. Do you think about what is being said?	5	4	3	2	1

COMPREHENSION	Almost Always	Occasionally		Almost Never	
11. Do you try to understand what the speaker means?	5	4	3	2	1
12. Do you try to understand why the speaker is trying to communicate?		5	4	3	2 1
13. Do you let the speaker finish what he is trying to say?	5	4	3	2	1
14. If the speaker hesitates, do you encourage him to go on?	5	4	3	2	1
15. Do you restate what is said to check your understanding?	5	4	3	2	1

EVALUATION

	Almost Always	Occasionally		Almost Never	
16. Do you withhold judgement about ideas until the speaker has finished?	5	4	3	2	1
17. Do you listen, regardless of the manner of speaking and choice of words?		5	4	3	2 1
18. Do you listen, even though you anticipate what the speaker is going to say?		5	4	3	2 1
19. Do you question the speaker in order to get a full explanation of the ideas?	5	4	3	2	1
20. Do you ask the speaker to define technical or unfamiliar words he uses?	5	4	3	2	1

Your Total Score

Assessment

'If you scored less than 70, take time to study and practise the skills of good communication. If you scored over 70, you are probably a good listener already but it is important to pay particular attention to those areas where you scored three or less.'[23]

6. Read John's account of Jesus' encounter with the woman at the well (John 4:1ff). Analyse Jesus' carefronting as John remembers it.

7. What can you, personally, learn from this chapter?

10

FORGIVING AND BEING FORGIVEN

Coming close. Care-fronting. 'The theory sounds so liberating and healing but when you attempt to translate it into practice, it's a different story. Clashes create strong, impulsive emotions that sweep through us with the force of a tornado that leaves people dead in its wake, that hurls cars and houses out of its path, that fills the air with flying debris. Yes. It's not the clash itself that is so devastating – it's the emotions that it triggers: rage, the desire to retaliate, the determination to take revenge.'

That's a complaint I wrote to God while I was halfway through this book. I record it here because I do not want to give the impression that reconciliation is easy or that we can be changed overnight from the self-centred warmongers that we are to the selfless peace-makers we can become. Rather, I prefer to highlight the situation as it really is: that, to change the metaphor: we all walk around carrying deeply submerged, but potentially lethal, time-bombs, our own emotions, which can explode in the face of our relationships at any time. Consequently, life is one long learning curve that presents us with the challenge of changing and being changed, of forgiving and being forgiven: of listening to ourselves. If we cultivate the art of listening to ourselves, gradually we may find ourselves growing in the self-awareness for which we applauded Paul in earlier chapters. Certain of Paul's reactions refused to die, as we have seen. They consequently caused endless problems: 'When I want to do good, evil is right there with me . . . In my mind [I] am a slave to God's law, but in the sinful nature a slave to the law of sin (Rom 7:21, 25).

If genuine reconciliation is to take place between those with whom we have clashed and ourselves, it is imperative that we, too, cultivate this self-awareness for 'in conflict, it is essential that both sides recognise their own part in the strife'.[1]

Instinctive reactions

When we *do* become aware of *our* part, we may well be forced to admit that our instinctive reaction to clashes with others is to pin the blame on the other party. In chapter three, for example, we placed the binoculars on Pastor Paul and observed how he did just this. He projected onto his colleague Jeremy all the blame for the disintegrating relationship that resulted in splitting the fellowship they led right down the middle. As we observed in chapter five, many of us fall into this trap much of the time. I have caught myself in the very act over and over again while I have been writing this book. Church leaders can do it, too. 'They're always bickering,' they may complain of their congregations. While the record of their complaints goes round and round, the needle seems to get stuck in a groove. Such people often seek, not to grow but only to groan. Instead of pursuing ways of ensuring that complaints result in a more rounded ministry that makes an impact on a wider section of the congregation, they add to the backbiting and bickering by blaming and accusing their critics. In this way they further succeed in marginalising and alienating their opponents further and end up using them as scapegoats.

Instead of or as well as resorting to projection, that is, piling blame on our opponent, we sometimes play a slightly different game. Instead of denying all personal responsibility by protesting: '*You're* the one who's bickering,' we admit and own our feelings while, at the same time, still heaping the blame on someone else. 'It's your fault that I get angry.' 'I am the way I am because you make me that way.' If Kevin Ford is representing his own generation accurately, as we noted in chapter five, the Buster generation clearly does just this when they claim:

> We are the ones who were not aborted or contracepted out of existence. We are the ones . . . who arrived just as the world was 'going bust' . . . We blame the generations of our parents and grandparents . . . for leaving us a social, economic and environmental mess to fix . . . We've grown up in an age of social malaise, urban decline, inept government, corrupt government, ineffective school systems, soaring national debt . . .[2]

In other words, it's all your fault that we are the way we are. The Buster generation goes even further. As well as transferring the blame for their behaviour on previous generations, they excuse themselves by rationalising – that is, they produce plausible, persuasive reasons why they should be exonerated from blame claiming: 'Any person in their right mind would excuse us for giving up on the world as it is at the moment.' While I was preparing to write this book, I heard a radio programme that summed up the situation well. Describing the Buster generation, the programme's presenter used a sentence that has stuck in my mind: 'They become villains to avoid becoming victims.' In other words, their view of society is such that they believe they will be marginalised or oppressed or victimised in some way. To protect themselves from this eventuality, they become the aggressor but in doing so, they rationalise, even excuse their aggressive behaviour. Busters, of course, are not the only ones to behave in this way. Many of us do it often. We do it

every time we protest: 'You make me mad when . . . '
We do it every time we pray that prayer that has no
answer: 'Lord when are you going to change that other
person so that our relationship can improve?' We do it
every time we protest, 'I may have been in the wrong
but I wasn't the only one.'

Some seemingly sweet people rarely blame or
accuse in the way I have described. Instead, they suppress from their conscious awareness the intense, terrifying, overpowering emotions that threaten to devour
them. They camouflage them with a beatific but plastic
smile. Vainly, they trust in the slogans, 'Out of sight,
out of mind. Out of mind, out of operation.'

I've decided to forget about it – I'm past caring
now,' one such person said to me recently, referring to
a relationship that has slowly and painfully reached
sdemise. 'Past caring . . .?' The tone of her voice and the
pain in her eyes betrayed her real feelings. They
revealed just how much she *did* care. Within a few
weeks, again she was denying that the problem even
existed. 'I am *not* angry,' she insisted in a tone of voice
that, together with the look on her face, clearly gave the
game away. Nothing had changed except that the gulf
between her and the person she was at variance with
had widened. Although she was valiantly attempting
to bury her feelings, they were being buried alive. She
was unwittingly adding her name to the long list of the
church's tormented Christians.

Being forgiven

Close by the Sea of Galilee, Jesus once encountered a
man who was similarly tormented. 'What is your
name?' Jesus asked. Jesus was not asking the man what
his parents had called him at his Naming ceremony.
Rather, he was commanding the evil spirits that were
driving the man to identify themselves. They did. 'My
name is Legion,' the man replied, 'for we are many'

(Mark 5:9). Just as that man was oppressed and possessed by evil spirits, so we are oppressed, often possessed, by compulsions which, though not demonic in the sense in which the man Mark mentions was possessed, nevertheless express themselves with demonic force. Like the man in Mark's story, we need the kind of encounter with Jesus that will cleanse, heal and release us from these enemies of the soul. The first step towards such inner freedom is to respond to Jesus' care-fronting question: 'What is *your* name?' The reason why that question requires a reply is that, when we give emotions a name, as we saw in chapters two and six, it is rather like giving a pan a handle. It suddenly becomes manageable instead of being too hot to handle. If we refuse or are unable to answer the question, though, such is the extent of God's love that he will gradually reveal the full picture to us in his own way and his own time – that is, at a time when we are ready to receive and respond. He came to one person, for example, in a dream:

In that place between wakefulness and dreams, I found myself in the room. There were no distinguishing features save for one wall covered with small index card files that stretched from floor to ceiling and seemingly endlessly in either direction. They all had very different headings.

As I drew near the wall of files, the first to catch my attention was one that read 'People I have Liked'. I opened it and began flipping cards. I quickly shut it, shocked to realise that I recognised the names written on each one. And then, without being told, I knew exactly where I was. This lifeless room with its small files was a crude catalogue system of my life. Here were written the actions of every moment, big and small, in a detail my memory couldn't match.

A sense of wonder and curiosity, coupled with horror, stirred within me as I began randomly opening files and exploring their content. Some brought joy and sweet memories; others a sense of shame and regret so intense that I would look over my shoulder to see if anyone was watching.

A file named: 'Friends' was next to one marked 'Friends I have Betrayed.' The titles ranged from the mundane to the outright weird. 'Books I have Read', 'Lies I have Told', 'Comfort I have Given', 'Jokes I have Laughed At'. Some were almost hilarious in their exactness: 'Things I have Yelled at my Brothers'. Others I couldn't laugh at: 'Things I have Done in my Anger', 'Things I have Muttered At My Parents Under My Breath'. I never ceased to be surprised by the contents. Often there were many more cards than I expected. Sometimes fewer than I hoped.

I was overwhelmed by the sheer volume of the life I had lived. Could it be possible that I had the time in my short life to write each of these thousands or even millions of cards? But each card confirmed this truth. Each was written in my own handwriting. Each signed with my own signature.

When I came to a file marked 'Lustful Thoughts', I felt a chill run through my body. I pulled the file out only an inch, not willing to test its size, and drew out a card. I shuddered at its detailed content. I felt sick to think that such a moment had been recorded. An almost animal rage broke on me. One thought dominated my mind: No one must ever see these cards! I have to destroy them! No one must ever see this room! In an insane frenzy I yanked the file out. Its size didn't matter now. I had to empty it and burn the cards.

But as I took it at one end and began pounding it on the floor, I could not dislodge a single card. I became desperate and pulled out a card, only to find it as strong as steel when I tried to tear it.

Defeated and utterly helpless, I returned the file to

its slot. Leaning my forehead against the wall, I let out a long, self-pitying sigh. And then I saw it. The title bore, 'People I have Shared the Gospel With.' The handle was brighter than those around it, newer, almost unused. I pulled on its handle and a small box not more than three inches long fell into my I could count the cards it contained on one hand. And then the tears came. I began to weep. Sobs so deep that the hurt started in my stomach and shook through me. I fell on my knees and cried. I cried out of the overwhelming shame of it all. The rows of file shelves swirled in my tear-filled eyes. No one must ever, ever know of this room. I must lock it up and hide the key.

But then, as I pushed away the tears, I saw Him. No, please, not Him. Not here. Oh, anyone but Jesus. I watched helplessly as He began to open the files and read the cards. I couldn't bear to watch His response. And in the moments I could bring myself to look at His face, I saw a sorrow deeper than my own. He seemed intuitively to go to the worst boxes. Why did He have to read every one?

Finally He turned and looked at me from across the room. He looked at me with pity in His eyes. But this was a pity that didn't anger me. I dropped my head, covered my face with my hands and began to cry again. He walked over and put His arm around me. He could have said so many things. But He didn't say a word. He just cried with me.

Then He got up and walked back to the wall of files. Starting at one end of the room, He took out a file and, one by one, began to sign His name over mine on each card.

'No!', I shouted rushing to Him. All I could find to say was, 'No, No', as I pulled the card from Him. His name shouldn't be on these cards. But there it was, written in red so rich, so dark, so alive. The name of Jesus covered mine. It was written with His blood.

He gently took the card back. He smiled a sad smile and began to sign the cards. I don't think I'll ever understand how He did it so quickly, but the next instant it seemed I heard Him close the last file and walk back to my side. He placed His hand on my shoulder and said, 'It is finished.' I stood up, and He led me out of the room. There was no lock on its door. There were still cards to be written.[3]

'He placed his hand on my shoulders.' In his unforgettable self-portrait, *The Return of the Prodigal*, Rembrandt paints the Father in Jesus' parable resting his hands on the prodigal's shoulders. Reflecting on that part of the picture, Henri Nouwen writes: 'The touch of his hands . . . seeks only to heal . . . His only desire is to bless.'[4]

'From the beginning of creation [God] has stretched out his arms in merciful blessing, never forcing himself on anyone, but always waiting . . . always hoping that his children will return so that he can speak words of love to them . . . The Father wants simply to let them know that the love they have searched for in such distorted ways has been, is, and always will be there for them . . . Those hands 'have held me from the hour of my conception . . . welcomed me at my birth, held me close to my mother's breast, fed me, and kept me warm. They have protected me in times of danger and consoled me in times of grief . . . Those hands are God's hands.'[5]

When we have experienced for ourselves the awesome mystery of such undeserved love, of such unearned and undeserved forgiveness, of such deep-down, through-and-through cleansing, we draw near to that place where we are willing to make an honest and humble confession. We stand on the threshold of renouncing and repenting of our prejudices and projections, our denial and our compulsions. We may yet regress because something may happen that prompts us to act like the kitten I once watched approach a swimming pool. Boldly, it approached the still, blue water. As it came closer, though, a ripple ruffled the surface so, instead of stopping to drink, the kitten took fright and fled. Even though fear might fill us, even though fear might add wings to our feet as we approach the loving God, given time, we will honour our resolve: to confess – that vital component of any peacemaking process.

Confession and Repentance

'There can be no reconciliation without confession,' claims David Cormack.[6] When two people clash, *both* act inappropriately or unwisely or unkindly. Such mutual hurting may have been unintentional but it happened. Both therefore need to make themselves vulnerable by admitting, 'I helped to create this conflict. I see now that I did this and this, I said that and that, I failed to say this, that and the other, I neglected to do such and such. In these and other ways *I* contributed to the escalation of this *impasse*.' In other words, confession concerns itself with telling another the truth about *ourselves* rather than telling others the truth about *themselves* – whether we spell out that truth in love or in hate. As Edwina Gateley puts it in *I Hear a Seed Growing:* 'I cannot meet the darkness of others until I have met my own darkness.'[7]

But, of course, as the De-escalation Curve on p 188 shows, although confession brings us one notch nearer that place where we can genuinely value the differences that once divided us from another, before reconciliation can take place, we need, not only to confess our part of the conflict but to repent of it also. To repent does not simply mean to say, 'I'm sorry'. Neither does it simply mean to feel full of remorse. To repent means, to do a U turn, to turn our back on the past and to resolve to live differently. To repent means to seek a radical change of heart that affects our attitude and behaviour. To repent means to resolve to stop – stop the bickering, stop the backbiting, stop the blaming, stop the projecting, stop the rationalising. To live differently. I do not repent on condition that my opponent repents also. I repent because, before God, I have become convinced that I have wronged another in thought and word and action and because, leaning heavily on God's grace and given a great deal of time, I am convinced that I can change and be changed. Repentance, then, is another vital factor in any peace-making process.

Healing

Although repentance is crucial to the resolution of conflict, before reconciliation can take place, repentance must be accompanied by healing.

Has anyone demonstrated this more powerfully than Rhiannon Lloyd and her colleague, Kristine Bresser, in their reconciliation work in Rwanda? Arriving in the country in the aftermath of the 1994 genocide, they faced the challenge of ministering hope to both Tutsi and Hutu Christians. How were they to accomplish this given the scale of the suffering that formed the back-cloth to their task?

'I've lost my whole family . . .', said some Tutsis they met. 'I've lost my whole village,' claimed others. 'I lost one hundred members of my extended family,' confided one pastor, 'now there's only one left and they maimed her.'

How could two mere foreigners minister hope in the middle of such hopelessness to people who, understandably, resisted the word 'reconciliation'? 'How do you expect us to be reconciled when we have suffered so much?' was their understandable protest.

Rhiannon and Kristine began by recognising and acknowledging what reconciliation is *not*. Reconciliation is *not* saying, 'OK, we'll all be friends now – just forget everything that happened – smother it with a blanket.' To invite shocked, suffering, traumatised, grief-stricken people to think along those lines would be asking the impossible. Instead, they realised that the word 'forgiveness' should not even pass their lips until they had taken both Tutsis and Hutus by the hand, as it were, and led them to Jesus, the healer of our hearts.

Picture the scene: a three-day seminar where the participants come from warring tribes; participants who have recently witnessed loved ones being butchered to death; people who have been betrayed by those they felt they could trust; people who have lost everything: land and livelihood – and even the desire to live. Imagine their reaction as a Welsh woman lays the foundation for healing by encouraging them to remember what they had seen and heard and felt during the war and then asking a heart-stopping, mind-bending question:

'Where was God in the trauma?'

Try to put yourself into their sandals as they struggle to respond to three questions Rhiannon scribbles on a large piece of paper stuck onto the crumbling walls with sellotape.

- Is everything that happens in the world the will of God? (By this she meant, is everything that happens in the world what God ideally wants?)
- If God is all-loving, why does he permit the innocent to suffer?
- If God is all-powerful, why doesn't he intervene and stop evil people doing evil things?

Imagine the puzzled, animated and pertinent discussion such questions spark off as individuals respond to them in buzz groups that are made up of both Hutus and Tutsis. Feel the tension as a sharp division of opinion rises to the surface: some people blaming God for the genocide, others blaming Satan, a few blaming human lust for power. Imagine the impact

Rhiannon makes when she drops into this seething ferment the suggestion that, just as God's heart had been full of grief when he witnessed the way his people pursued the inclinations of their own hearts before the Flood (Gen 6:6), so God's heart is now full of pain over the strife that had caused Tutsis and Hutus to hate and massacre one another; that just as Jesus once wept over Jerusalem crying, 'O Jerusalem, Jerusalem . . . how often I have longed to gather your children together, as a hen gathers her chicks under her wings, but you were not willing' (Matt 23:37), so now he is weeping over Rwanda crying, 'Oh! Rwanda, Rwanda . . . If only . . . ' Imagine their response to her insistence that they should focus on *God's* feelings and listen to *God's* heartbeat.

Try to tune into the atmosphere that now electrifies the room as person after person perceives that God really cares for each individual in Rwanda; that, far from being the perpetrator of the genocide, in a very real sense, the last thing God wanted for these people was war and pain, grief and suffering. Picture them as the proverbial penny drops and they realise that, just as they continue to weep, God weeps with them and for them and over them. Sense how a flicker of hope is fanned into a flame as they acknowledge that this weeping God is also the sovereign God who can redeem every human tragedy. Look at the hopelessness through their eyes and see how these revelations pave the way for their hearts to hear and understand that life-changing claim of Isaiah's: Surely He has borne 'our *griefs* and carried our *sorrows*' (Is 53:4, NKJV, emphasis mine).

Sense how their hearts are being prepared to accept that, on the cross, Jesus dealt, not only with our sinfulness but also with our woundedness. In his own body, he carried, not only our guilt but our griefs – including our tragedies. Just as Jesus begs us to transfer our sins onto him so that he can become our *sin*-bearer, so he begs us to entrust our pain to him so that he can become our *pain*-bearer. From the cross, it is as though he cries, 'Let me do the hurting for you. I want to bear the searing pain that pierces your heart – including the pain that has been inflicted on you by the sinfulness of others.'

Try to tune into the changed atmosphere in the seminar now that hearts are being softened by the water of God's Spirit. Tune in, too, to the inner conflict that tears many of the listeners apart as they struggle, on the one hand, with the challenge to name their hurt and, on the other hand, with their culture's resistance to emotional openness. Feel the inner tension as many hear Rhiannon insist, 'If Jesus is to become our pain-bearer, first we must acknowledge rather than hide the fact that we have been hurt. We need to talk – maybe to cry,' while, all their lives their mentors have drummed into them the opposite: 'If someone hurts you, laugh. Don't let them know you are vulnerable. They might use it against you.'

'Ask yourself, "What is the worst experience I've ever encountered?" Think about it. Write about it.' Imagine the impact that suggestion makes on these people who have been torn to shreds by suffering. Watch them write. Listen as Rhiannon invites them to share their experiences with one or two others. Sense their dilemma as those who have been culturally conditioned to conceal rather than to reveal their pain consider whether or not to comply. Look at their faces while Rhiannon summarises with a sentence on another piece of paper stuck on the wall the atrocities they now describe. Listen and watch while, gently, she asks: 'What does God feel about all this?' Observe how she speaks God's good news into the situation by taking in her hand a red pen with which she proceeds to draw across the paper a huge, red cross. Observe their faces as they hear her say: 'This is the only place I know where we can take all this pain. This is the place where, not only can we lay our own sin but all the sins that have ever been committed against us.'

Fix the eyes of your imagination onto this sobered group as she invites them to stand. Hear her invite them to tell God 'what you saw. Tell him what it did to you. If you are angry, tell him. If you're full of despair, tell him. If emotions rise, don't hold them back. Know that if you start to weep, God is weeping with you.'

Peep at these deeply suffering people weeping and wailing as they pour out to God the full extent of their pain. Feel their anguish. Hear them sing in their own language:

What a friend we have in Jesus
All our sins and griefs to bear;
What a privilege to carry
Everything to God in prayer.

Watch them pray for one another as a rough, five-foot wooden cross is carried into the room and placed on the floor together with a hammer and a pile of nails. Hear Rhiannon seal her teaching with this powerful visual aid. Hear her invite any who might find it helpful to come forward to that cross and to nail on it the pieces of paper on which they have written the record of some of their sufferings. Marvel at the symbolism as you hear the hammer of the nails that are securing their pieces of paper to the crude cross. Then watch person after person, having nailed their paper to the tree, return to their seats singing spontaneously songs that exalt the cross of Jesus. Listen while these African Christian leaders respond to one final question: 'Was God still at work in the middle of your greatest darkness? Does anyone here have evidence that his Holy Spirit was at work while you were caught up in the atrocities that caused you so much suffering?' Picture their faces as you ponder some of the responses:

'We heard people praying for those who were hack-

236

ing them to death.'

'We saw Hutus hiding Tutsis in the roof of their homes even though they would have been killed if they had been caught.'

Watch these brave people leave the seminar – to file into the final seminar the next day. Listen again as they respond to yet another of Rhiannon's probing questions: 'Does anyone have any feed-back from yesterday's seminar?' Witness the way God has worked:

'My heart is changed since I gave my pain to Jesus. I can forgive now.'

'My heart is different today. Yesterday, I was full of hatred. Today I feel full of love. It was giving my pain to Jesus that brought about the change. When I saw that Jesus was carrying all my pain and carrying all their sin against me, then I found my heart was light and he filled me with joy. Then I found I could forgive.'

Assimilate the implications of these testimonies as Rhiannon expresses them: 'Before wounded people can be expected to forgive, a place must be provided where they can face the pain, talk about their wounds and experience God's healing touch.' *Then* from the wellsprings of their own heart, the grace to forgive will flow like a cleansing stream.

Such healing cannot be hurried. It takes time. As we have seen, on occasions, God can and does accelerate the healing process. More often than not, however, the pain of years takes years to heal. On the island where I live, for example, people who lost relatives and friends in the 1974 bloodshed still live with the anguish of not knowing whether their loved ones are alive or dead. Healing for such pain is rarely Often it comes drip by drip over a long period of time. Or I think of the countless women who have carried around in their hearts from childhood the secret shame and pain they suffered at the hands of a father who sexually abused them. Many want to forgive and feel frustrated because the healing that is the prerequisite for forgiving seems to come oh, so slowly and, as David Augsburger reminds us: 'When "forgiveness" denies that there is anger, acts as if it never happened, smiles as though it never hurt, fakes as though it's all forgotten – Don't offer Don't trust it. Don't depend on it. It's not forgiveness, it's magical fantasy.'[8]

Forgive

Instead of embarking on such a fantasy trip, many keep their integrity and express, instead, the battle that rages inside them:

'Forgive . . .?
Me?
Them . . . ?

I can't Lord.
Can't do it.

Do I want to?
Do I . . .?
Not even sure of that Lord.
Feel muddled.

Seems so hard.
Why should I forgive?
They have hurt me
so much.

They have taken everything
That is mine.
And left me lying
In the dirt.

All I can say is
'Lord, help me to want to want
To forgive.

And then –
You do the rest Lord –
You do the rest.'[9]

The author of that prayer-poem is all too aware of the far-reaching implications of forgiveness. She knows that 'to forgive' does not mean 'to forget', 'to excuse', 'to pretend it never happened'. The Greek word for 'to forgive' is *aphesis* which means 'to drop', 'to let go of', 'to relinquish'.

I have often heard the cliché 'forgive and forget'. I cringe every time I hear it because it misrepresents the true nature of forgiveness. When we forgive, we drop, not the memory of the conflict in which we have been embroiled but the bitterness and the resentment and the hatred that we have harboured in our hearts. When Jesus cried his heart-rending prayer from the cross: 'Father forgive', he was not begging his Father to *forget* the sin of the world, neither was he, himself, seeking to forget that he was encircled by those who wished him only harm. No. Far from forgetting, he remained acutely aware of the world's plight and mankind's treachery in all its stark reality. From a remembered pain-racked place, still he pleaded: 'Father, forgive . . .', What did he mean by this cry: 'Father drop the punishment they have earned'? Or, 'Father, set *me* free from bondage to their hurt. Set me free from any desire to punish. Set me free to drop any cloying resentment that clogs my memory and prevents me from dying in their place.' Jesus alone knows what he meant when he prayed this prayer of forgiveness. Jesus alone knew that he was not pleading with a God who answered that prayer with reluctance because he hates mankind. On the contrary, Jesus knew that he was conversing with a holy Father who, because of his purity, cannot countenance sin, yet continues to love the world he created *and* the people who inhabit it; a Father who was more than ready to avert the death penalty that sin warranted.

The opposite of 'to drop', is 'to cling'. When hurt has been inflicted on us by those we trusted, our reflex action is to respond with a resolve like: 'I'll *never* forgive him for that . . .' Bishop Stephen Verney reminds us that 'we are in bondage to what we cling to'. Illustrating this on one occasion, as he spoke to a group of clergy on the subject of forgiveness, he clung to the reading desk on the platform from which he was speaking. 'When I cling to this desk,' he exclaimed, 'I put myself in bondage to it. I can take two or three steps back, two or three steps to my left and two or three steps to my right but I am not free to walk further. I will only be really free when I *aphesis* – when I let go. If I decide to let go, not only do I set myself free, I also set the desk free to be the useful thing it was created to be.'

Was this the point Jesus was trying to make at the grave of Lazarus when he used the word *aphesis* as he addressed the awe-struck bystanders who had witnessed Lazarus emerge from the tomb where he had been incarcerated for four days? 'Unloose him and let him go,' Jesus instructs them. That is, remove the grave-clothes that still bind him and prevent him from walking away from his grave. The word he uses for 'let him go' is the word we have been placing under the microscope: *aphesis* – to drop, to let go, to be released from.

The implication is, then, that a whole variety of challenges are wrapped up in this one word 'forgive'. First comes the challenge to let go of bitterness and hatred and resentment, as we have seen. Next comes the challenge to release myself by unwinding from my opponents the bandages of death that I have wound round them like a web: letting go of my desire that they should leave the church, maybe; letting go by switching off the record that plays endlessly the din of my complaints; letting go by renouncing the longing that they should disappear from my life, the determination to push them out of my mind, the wish, perhaps, that they should even drop dead. Forgiveness also presents us with a far-reaching challenge: the challenge to commit ourselves to a renewed relationship with the person with whom we have been locked in conflict. Such a relationship will remember past pain, learn its lessons well while, at the same time, resolutely turning its back on the past as it faces the future determining to act and react differently.

In other words, 'forgiveness' faces us with a series of choices: to groan or to grow; to let go or to cling; to play tit-for-tat or to seek real and lasting reconciliation – or, as the writer of the prayer-poem I have quoted is doing, to have the integrity to admit to reality: the bitter war that rages within that prompts part of our personality to capitulate and the other part to insist: 'I *can't* forgive – . . . why should I?'

Steps to forgiveness

No matter which of these three choices we make, if we are to move forward, the way ahead is the same. The first step is to admit the truth, at least to ourselves:

- I have been sinned against.
- I am hurting.
- There is a sense in which I have a right to retaliate – to punish (Ex 21:23–25).
- I therefore stand on the threshold of one of the most important decisions I have ever made: to step out of the realm of rights and into the realm of grace or to insist on my rights and live in the light of them.

In order to make a considered rather than a reckless choice, the next step, far from forgetting the incident, is to remember it in all its ugliness or sordidness, its pain and gory detail. Some will re-connect with the memory best by writing about it. Others may find they need a friend, a mentor or a counsellor with whom they can share such confidentialities.

Having recalled the grim steps that resulted in the relationship at best turning sour and, at worst, ending in betrayal or breakdown, the next step is to pause, to turn the spotlight on myself, to trace my own journey through life so far, to plot onto the map the way I have travelled, places where *I* have failed, places where I have experienced the freely-given grace and forgiveness of God – to recall *these* times in all their bittersweet vividness.

While we bask in these memories, we then ask ourselves the question: 'Just as God forgave me, just as God let me go free, relinquishing his right to punish me, will I relinquish my rights or *will* I, instead, cling to them?' At this stage, we may still be smarting, still be full of fear. That is why I have emphasised the word *will* several times. The choice that faces us has little do with feelings that may well still be bruised and confused and battered. It relies heavily on an act of the will.

If our will says, 'Yes. Go for it . . .', we let go of the bitterness and the resentment, the hatred and the jealousy that have been eating us up.

As we have already seen in this chapter, it helps some to enact this letting go. I sometimes go to the beach near my home to do this. There, I pick up a pebble that seems to represent by its shape and size the feelings that I have resolved to drop. When I have found the kind of stone I am searching for, I seek to be conscious of God's presence as well as the emotions that I know I must drop. When I am connected, as it were, with God and my feelings, when I am as certain as I can be that, with integrity, I really can let go, I drop my stone, listening, with relief to its 'plop'. At other times, I hurl my rock into the sea, recalling those wonderful words the psalmist penned: 'As far as the east is from the west, so far has he removed our transgressions from us' (Ps 103:12).

There are times, though, when, having found 'my' stone, I struggle. Like the author of the prayer-poem I quoted, I reach the conclusion: 'I can't . . . not yet.' When ministering on one occasion to someone who had suffered the indignity of sexual abuse, God seemed to show me what a beautiful prayer this is in his eyes. The young woman who was confiding in me expressed her deep longing to forgive her father for consistently abusing her throughout her formative years. 'But I can't . . .', she confessed. 'Not yet . . .' 'But, Lord, I am willing to be made willing,' she prayed a little later. And she wept – beautiful tears, the pain of years. As she wept, I wept too and I sensed I saw God weeping. He saw. He heard. He understood. He was willing to wait. He was not in a hurry. He heard, not simply the words that were being uttered but the words this woman will one day pray when her healing is complete: 'Father forgive . . . he didn't know the extent of the hurt he was inflicting on me.'

Frequency of forgiveness

'How often must I forgive?' Was Peter exasperated when he blurted out his question to Jesus? The Greek suggests that the question he was actually asking is one many of us have asked time and time again: 'How often must I forgive the same person for the same thing? Seven times?' Seven sounds such a generous number in the circumstances. Does Jesus chuckle, I wonder, as he responds: 'Seven . . . Try seventy times seven' – by which time, it is to be hoped, we shall have lost count and forgiving that person for that particular thing will have become a gentle, gracious habit. Maybe, by this time, too, we shall have found countless ways of expressing the fact that we really have relinquished our rights and dropped any bitterness, for forgiveness seeks to discover ways of blessing the person who has hurt or offended us. Depending on the nature of the altercation, this might be a love-note on a spouse's pillow, an unexpected but welcome phone-call, fax or e-mail, an un-birthday card or present, a special meal lovingly prepared. Or it might be a poem or prayer that pierces as many hearts and brings tears to as many eyes as this one that was penned following the brutal murder of the author's son:

O God
We remember, not only our son, Bahran
  but also his murderers.

Not because they killed him in the prime of his youth
  and made our hearts bleed and our tears flow;

Not because with this savage act they have brought
  further disgrace on the name of our country
  among the civilised nations of the world;

But because, through their crime, we now follow
  Thy footsteps more closely in the way of sacrifice.

The terrible fire of this calamity burns up all
  selfishness and possessiveness in us;

Its flame reveals the depth of depravity
  and meanness and suspicion,
  the dimension of hatred
  and the measure of sinfulness in human nature;

It makes obvious as never before our need to trust in
  God's love as shown in the Cross of Jesus
  and His Resurrection;

Love which makes us free from hate
  toward our persecutors;

Love which brings patience, forbearance, courage,
    loyalty,
  humility, generosity, greatness of heart;

Love which more than ever deepens our trust in
    God's final victory
  and His eternal designs for the Church and for the
    world;

Love which teaches us how to prepare ourselves to
    face our own day of death.

O God,

Our son's blood has multiplied the fruit of the Spirit
  in the soil of our souls:

So when the murderers stand before Thee
  on the day of Judgement

Remember the fruit of the Spirit by which
  they have enriched our lives,

And forgive.[10]

The spin-off of forgiveness

Our way of blessing someone who has hurt us might
take the form of a quest like Kim's.

Kim Phuc's claim to fame came when she was just
nine years old. Then, she was an ordinary Vietnamese
village girl. On June 5th, 1972, however, she sustained
third-degree burns to two-thirds of her body when her
village became the target of an American napalm
bombing raid. On June 6th, the world woke to be
shocked, stunned and touched by the photograph of
Kim that stared out at them from their morning newspapers: Kim, racing naked and terror-stricken down
the road from her village screaming, 'It's hot! It's so
hot!' – meaning her body was so hurt from the burns.

Despite her horrendous injuries, against all the
odds, miraculously, Kim recovered. Subsequently, she
not only came to faith, she embarked on a mission of
forgiveness and reconciliation. She also embarked on a
quest – to meet face to face the man who had ordered

245

the attack. Her travels took her to groups of American students who listened wide-eyed as she told them how the man who had taken the photograph of her saved her life by giving her his own water flask to drink from; how he had poured water over her body to cool her down and how he had taken her to a hospital with a burns unit. The students not only wept with her, they received through her example and her testimony the ability, similarly, to forgive those who had hurt them in more minor ways.

Her travels took her, too, to another meeting in America where she described for the audience the events of her childhood, dwelling, not so much on the horror as on her longing to meet the pilot of the plane that had dropped the bombs that blasted her village. Little did she know that that man 'happened' to be in the audience. Little did she know that, since seeing in the newspapers the day after the attack a photograph of Kim, with the skin falling off her badly-burned body, he had been riddled with guilt. Little did she know that, although he had subsequently become a Methodist minister, he was still so much in bondage to the past that he had become an alcoholic and suffered several broken marriages. Little did she know that this tormented man was listening to her say: 'I'd like to meet the man who ordered the attack and tell him I forgive him.'

After the meeting, the pilot met Kim backstage. When he introduced himself to her, Kim looked him in the eyes and with integrity and genuineness spoke out those words that had welled up from her heart years earlier: 'I forgive you.' His response was one of, heartfelt relief and great gratitude: 'It's as though the weight of years has rolled off me. I really needed to see you look me in the eyes and to hear you say those words, "I forgive you." '

Because Kim was willing to forgive the one who had made of her a war victim, the pilot of the plane was set free to forgive himself for an act that had killed and maimed countless innocent people. Such is the power of forgiveness.

When we forgive someone who has hurt or offended or insulted us; someone who has, perhaps, ruined our reputation in some way, we not only set them free, we swing open the door to another miracle: the door that enables us to see the eyes of Jesus focused on us as they once focused on the woman caught committing adultery that we looked at in an earlier chapter. We open the door to hearing the voice of God whispering *to us*, 'I do not condemn you . . . I forgive *you*.'

When we forgive, we reap yet another wonderful reward that Jesus hints at in the Lord's Prayer and that he spells out elsewhere:

- Forgive us our sins as we forgive those who sin against us (Matt 6:12; Luke 11:4).
- 'If you forgive men when they sin against you, your heavenly Father will also forgive you' (Matt 6:14).
- 'Forgive, and you will be forgiven' (Luke 6:37).
- When you pray, 'if you have anything against someone, *forgive*' – then your heavenly Father will 'wipe your slate clean of sins' (Mark 11:25, *The Message*).

When we refuse to forgive or while we struggle to forgive in the way I described earlier in this chapter squealing, 'I can't . . . not yet'; whether we realise it or not, poison pours into our hearts and pollutes our lives: the poison of hatred and bitterness, resentment and jealousy. Our hearts harden. When we genuinely forgive, that is, when we let go of the grudge we bear another, it is as though the divine surgeon comes *to us*, lances this abscess of the heart and bids us watch while the pus and the poison pour out of us. Can there be any greater gift or more wonderful release than this cauterisation of our innermost being?

Now both we and the person we have hated are gloriously free to stand at the foot of Christ's cross and receive his cleansing and a fresh inflow of his healing love.

Suggested exercises

I have written much of this book in the mountains of Cyprus. One of my delights has been to walk through the pine trees each morning before sunrise and to gaze at the still-dark mountain peaks with their equally dark forested slopes. As I've watched, the sun has kissed the highest peak and slowly and steadily spread its light onto first one mountain slope, then another, then another.

One morning, an ancient pine tree that towered above me attracted my attention. The previous day it had been powdered with dust but an unseasonal shower had washed it clean. Now it stood silhouetted black against the cloudless blue sky until the rays of the rising sun touched the needles nearest heaven. While I watched, the golden ball beamed its light not only on the uppermost part of the tree, in the awesome silence it touched every up-turned needle and each cone: those that were closed and virgin green as well as those that were brown and worn, their faces wide open with wonder. While I stood gazing, the now-warm sun seemed also to penetrate each crevice and crack of the age-old tree trunk. The tree did nothing – except to be the tree it was created to be; except to receive the gift of another day; except to respond to the miracle of osmosis.

The tree and the landscape reminded me of my life that is so often soiled. 'I once likened myself to a vine,' I sensed the whisper of Jesus. 'Why don't you sometimes liken yourself to a pine tree? All you have to do is to stand there, just as you are: with parts of you fully matured, like wide-open pine cones, parts of you cracked and flaking like the tree's trunk, parts of you ready to drop off like some of those well-worn needles, parts of you still growing like those tightly-closed green cones. Why don't you admit, from time to time, that you are jaded, worse, covered with dust – not looking your best? Why don't you open every part of yourself to the gentleness of my showers with which I'll douche you? Why don't you hold up your arms to me, turn your face to me, open your heart and mind to me, give me access to every nook and cranny of your being that I might penetrate the depths and heights of your being as I penetrate and touch the tree before '

While I weighed and pondered these questions, some words of the psalmist winged their way into my heart: 'Search me, O God, and know my heart; test me and know my anxious thoughts. See if there is any offensive way in me, and lead me in the way everlasting' (Ps 139:23–24).

Since that moment, when I've been made aware of the need for cleansing, I have, indeed, likened myself to that tree. I have stood tall, trying to hide nothing but rather to expose everything to God. I have welcomed the ever-available but through and through washing he gives.

'But what about the pus and the poison?' I protested one day. 'Make an incision in my trunk,' I pleaded, 'so that, just as resin oozes out of pine trees, so all that pollutes me may pour out of me. Then, just as the trees' arms wave in the wind, blow on me by your Spirit and give me the grace to respond to your in-breathing.'

If, as you have been reading this chapter, you have become aware of the need to forgive, you might similarly like to pretend that you are a tree that is being washed and warmed and wind-blown as you allow God to minister to you. Alternatively, you might prefer to use the method I mentioned earlier in this chapter. Find a stone that symbolises, for you, the size and shape of the attitudes you want to let go of. Curl your

fingers around it. Be aware that this is a part of you.
Seek an awareness of the presence of God and when
you are ready, wherever you are – on the beach, in the
garden, in your kitchen, in the place where you pray, in
a church, kneeling in front of a cross, drop your stone.
Listen to its fall. Let it symbolise the fact that the attitude it represents has gone. Now, open the hand that
once clenched that bitterness or resentment or hatred
or desire for revenge. Hold it out to God and let him fill
it with his love for the person with whom you have
clashed.

And what if I can't drop my stone? What if my sense
of failure is so great that even God can't forgive me?
Such fears haunt countless Christians. 'Picture Jesus
hanging on the Cross', Gerard Hughes invites such
people in *God of Surprises*.[11] Recognise that he is hanging there encrusted by the sin of the whole world. Tell
him that you know that Isaiah's words are true when
he writes: 'The Lord has laid on him the iniquity of us
all' (Is 53:6).

Thank God for loving the world so much that he
sent his Son to save us from the kind of sin that weighs
you down. Then turn your face to the Crucified One
and challenge him: 'But you've met your match in me.
You may have carried to the cross the sin of the whole
world but I am the greatest of sinners. I know you can't
forgive me.' Can you say it? If not, why not? What can
you say instead? How do you feel as you gaze, as you
wriggle, as you struggle, as you deliberate?

We have seen how liberating it can be for us and for
others when we heed the words of Jesus:

'This is how I want you to conduct yourself . . . If
you enter your place of worship and, about to make an
offering, you suddenly remember a grudge a friend has
against you, abandon your offering, leave immediately, go to this friend and make things right. Then and
only then, come back and work things out with God'

(Matt 5:23,24, *The Message*).

The sobering fact is that most of us choose to ignore Jesus' salutary warnings:

- 'In prayer there is a connection between what God does and what you do. You can't get forgiveness from God, for instance, without also forgiving others. If you refuse to do your part, you cut yourself off from God's part' (Matt 6:15, *The Message*).

- 'Don't pick on people, jump on their failures, criticise their faults . . . Don't condemn those who are down; that hardness can boomerang. Be easy on people; you'll find life a lot easier' (Luke 6:37, *The Message*).

- 'If you forgive someone's sins, they're gone for good. If you don't forgive sins, what are you going to do with them?' (John 20:23, *The Message*); or as the NIV translates that verse:

- 'If you forgive anyone his sins, they are forgiven; if you do not forgive them, they are not forgiven.'

Are *you* holding a grudge against anyone? Are you hating anyone? Are *you* jumping on another's failures, criticising their faults, concentrating on the smudge on *their* face rather than on the fixed, ugly sneer that spoils your own? Re-read the teaching of Jesus that I have just quoted from John 20. Add to it Jesus' powerful parable that Matthew records in chapter 18 of his Gospel (v 18ff). Look into these passages in rather the same way as you would look in a mirror. What do you see? What is your heart-response? Listen to yourself for a whole week. Try to discern the answer to the following questions:

- When you clash with someone, what is your in-

stinctive reaction? Do you project blame onto the
other party?
- Do you transfer responsibility from yourself to
someone else?
- Do you excuse yourself by rationalising?
- Do you suppress your real feelings?
- Do you deny such feelings?

Will you perpetuate the pain that pierces the heart
of God when brothers bicker and friends fight,
when spouses spit at one another and church members criticise and castigate each other? Or will you
forgive – drop your accusations, let go of your hardness and receive such a measure of God's love for
those you dislike so much that you pray for them *in
love*?

Can you, will you, re-read the Steps to Forgiveness
section of this chapter and work it into your life in
rather the same way as we work yeast into a batch
of dough? Can you, will you, re-read Kim's story,
Bishop Dehqani-Tafti's prayer (see p 244) and the
account of the way the Holy Spirit touched and
healed hurting Hutu and Tutsi Christians? Can you,
will you, nail your griefs and grievances to the
cross? Can you, will you, regularly ask the Holy
Spirit to shine the torchlight of truth into the nooks
and crannies of your mind and heart, to show you
yourself? Can you, will you, ask God to give you the
grace to grow and to go on growing even though to
grow might take you along a tortuous path? Can
you, will you, play your part in ensuring that the
prayer of Jesus is answered in all your relationships:

> *'that all of them may be one, Father,*
> *just as you are in me*
> *and I am in you.'*
> *(John 17:21)*

NOTES

Preface
1. Edward de Bono. Quoted David Cormack, *Peacing Together* (Eastbourne: MARC,1989) p 9.

Chapter One
1. Justin Dennison, *Team Ministry* (London: Hodder & Stoughton, 1997) p 116.
2. Ibid pp 116–117. Emphasis mine.
3. Jim Packer. Source not traced.
4. Eugene Peterson's phrase.
5. J. Neuner SJ, *Walking With Him* (India, IHS, 1989) p 147.

Chapter Two
1. David Cormack, *Peacing Together* (MARC Europe, 1989) p 17, emphasis mine.
2. My adaptation of Frank Lake's model in *Clinical Theology* (London: DLT, 1966) p 205.
3. Henri Nouwen, *Reaching Out* (London: Fount, 1980) p 31.
4. Justin Dennison, *Team Ministry* (London: Hodder & Stoughton, 1996) p 121.
5. David Cormack's phrases.
6. Myra Chave-Jones, *Listening to Your Feelings* (Oxford: Lion, 1989) p 30.
7. Ibid p 14.
8. I am drawing here on the insights of Frank Lake, *Clinical Theology*, op. cit.
9. Graham Millar, *Prayer Search* (Melbourne: Joint Board of Christian Education, 1989) pp 10, 14.
10. David Cormack, op. cit. p 27.
11. Dr Vance L. Shepperson and Dr Bethyl Joy Shepperson, *Tracks in the Sand* (Nashville: Thomas Nelson and Son, 1992) pp 30, 31.

Chapter Three
1. David Cormack, *Peacing Together*, (MARC Europe, 1989) p 17.
2. Michael Green, *I Believe in Satan's Downfall* (London: Hodder & Stoughton, 1984) pp 26– 27.
3. Ibid p 24.
4. Ibid p 23.
5. David Cormack, *Peacing Together* op. cit. p 59.
6. Ibid p 83.
7. Eugene Peterson's phrases, *The Message*, p 398.
8. Ranald Macaulay and Jerram Barrs, *Christianity with a Human Face* (Leicester: IVP, 1978) p 96.
9. David Runcorn, *Touch Wood* (London: DLT, 1992) pp 55–56.

Chapter Four
1. I am here developing David Cormack's image that he describes in *Peacing Together* (MARC Europe, 1989) ch 3.
2. Lawrence J. Crabb, *The Marriage Builder* (New Malden: NavPress, 1987) p 35.
3. Ibid p 72.
4. Not their real names but a real situation.
5. Esther de Waal, *Seeking God* (London: Fount, 1984) p 76.
6. Ibid p 3, emphasis mine.
7. David Kiersey and Marilyn Bates, *Please Understand Me* (Del Mar: Gnosology Books Ltd, 1984) p 3.
8. Ibid p 3.
9. Quoted from a handout I was once given at a seminar. Source unknown.

Chapter Five
1. David R. Mace, *Success in Marriage* (London: Abingdon Press, 1985).
2. Kath Donovan, *The Pastoral Care of Missionaries* (Bible College of Victoria, no date) p 12.
3. Kevin Ford and Jim Denney, *Jesus for a New Generation* (London: Hodder & Stoughton, 1996) pp 8, 11, 18.
4. Ibid p 21.
5. Ibid, pp 24–27, 34, 35.
6. Kath Donovan, op. cit. p 11.
7. Kath Donovan, op. cit. p 12.
8. Kevin Ford with Jim Denney, op. cit. p 30.
9. Kath Donovan, op. cit. p 12.
10. Joyce Huggett, *Finding God in the Fast Lane* (Guildford: Eagle, 1993).
11. Marjory Foyle, 'Missionary Relationships: Powderkeg or Powerhouse' ch 37 of *Helping Missionaries Grow*, ed Kelly S. O'Donnell PsyD and Michele Lewis O'Donnell PsyD (Pasadena, California: William Carey Library, 1988) p 402.
12. I am drawing here on an article written by Dorothy Gish PhD (Prof Of Early Childhood and Family Life Education at Messiah College, Pennsylvania) published ibid ch 35.
13. Marjory Foyle, op. cit. p 402.
14. M. Scott-Peck, *The People of the Lie* (New York: Touchstone Books, 1983) p 74.
15. David Huggett's adaptation of David Cormack's Strife Curve, *Peacing Together* (MARC Europe, 1989) p 45.
16. David Cormack, op. cit. pp 43–44.

Chapter Six
1. David Augsburger, *Anger and Assertiveness in Pastoral Care* (Philadelphia: Fortress Press, 1979) p 4.
2. Ibid p 4.
3. Richard P. Walters, *Anger* (Leicester: IVP, 1983) p 21.
4. Ibid p 11.
5. Ibid p 16.
6. Ibid p 16.

7. David and Vera Mace, *Love and Anger in Marriage* (London: Marshall Pickering, 1982) p 32.
8. Ibid p 29.
9. Harriet Goldhor Lerner, *The Dance of Anger* (Wellingborough, Grapevine, 1990) p 1.
10. Richard Walters, op. cit. p 29.
11. David Augsburger, op. cit. p 20.
12. Ibid p 20.
13. Ibid p 21.
14. Richard Walters, op. cit. p 61.
15. David Augsburger, op. cit. p 22.
16. Myra Chave-Jones, *Listening to Your Feelings* (Oxford: Lion, 1989) p 112.
17. Harriet Goldhor Lerner's spelling.
18. Harriet Goldhor Lerner, op. cit. p 14.
19. David Mace in *Love and Anger in Marriage*, op. cit.   pp 13–14.

Chapter Seven
1. David Cormack, *Peacing Together* (MARC Europe, 1989) p 17.
2. Ibid p 26.
3. Ibid p 35.
4. My adaptation of a handout I was given at a seminar. Source unknown.
5. St Augustine, *Confessions viii*.
6. David Cormack, op. cit. p 101.
7.My adaptation of a handout I was given at a seminar. Source unknown.

Chapter Eight
1. David Cormack, *Peacing Together* (MARC Europe, 1989) p 79.
2. My slight adaptation of this well-loved prayer.
3. David and Vera Mace, *Love and Anger in Marriage* (London: Marshall Pickering, 1982) p 11.
4. Ibid p 14.
5. Ibid pp 12, 13, 16–18.
6. David Cormack, op. cit. p 85.
7. David Cormack, op. cit. p 85.
8. David Cormack, op. cit. p 85.
9. C. S. Lewis, *The Screwtape Letters* (London: Fontana, 1960) p 22.
10. David Huggett's adaptation of Robert McLeish's adaptation of David Cormack's diagram in *Peacing Together* op. cit. p 45.
11. David Cormack, op. cit. p 100.
12. Quoted *Union Life*, July/August 1992.
13. The contract is inspired by David and Vera Mace's *Love and Anger in Marriage* and *How to Have a Happy Marriage* as well as John and Agnes Sturts' *Marriage Enrichment Manual* (Auckland: Christian Care Centre, 1986).

Chapter Nine
1. David Cormack, *Peacing Together* (MARC Europe, 1989) p 103.
2. David Cormack's definition of sharing, ibid p 103.

3. Ibid p 103.
4. Ibid p 103.
5. David Cormack, *Team Spirit* (Eastbourne: MARC, 1987) p 88.
6. Ibid p 88.
7. Joyce Huggett, *Listening to Others* (London: Hodder & Stoughton, 1988).
8. David Cormack, *Team Spirit,* op. cit. p 88.
9. For a fuller description of this and the listening process see chapters 5 and 6 of *Listening to Others,* op. cit.
10. My adaptation of John and Agnes Sturt's diagram in *Marriage Enrichment Manual* (Auckland, Christian Care Centre, 1986) p 22.
11. John and Agnes Sturt, op. cit. p 23.
12. David Augsburger, *Caring Enough to Hear and Be Heard* (Scottdale, Philadelphia: Herald Press, 1982) p 29.
13. Anne Long, *Listening* (London: Daybreak, 1990) p 47.
14. David Cormack, *Team Spirit,* op. cit. p 90.
15. David Augsburger, *Caring Enough to Confront* (London: Marshall Pickering, 1985) pp 52, 54.
16. Michael Jacobs. Quoted Anne Long, *Listening,* op. cit. p 42.
17. I am drawing here on the insights of David Augsburger in *Caring Enough to Confront,* op. cit. p 9.
18. Ibid pp 10, 11.
19. David Augsburger, op. cit. p 53.
20. Ibid p 50.
21. Inspired by Mapping the Conflict – an exercise devised by The Conflict Resolution Network, NSW Australia.
22. David Augsburger, op. cit. p 52.
23. David Cormack, *Team Spirit,* op. cit. pp 86, 87.
24. Culled from David Augsburger, op. cit. p 59.

Chapter Ten

1. David Cormack, *Peacing Together* (MARC Europe, 1989) p 60.
2. Kevin Ford and Jim Denney, *Jesus for a New Generation* (London: Hodder & Stoughton, 1996) p 8.
3. Author unknown.
4. Henri Nouwen, *The Return of the Prodigal* (London: DLT, 1992) p 90.
5. Ibid p 91.
6. David Cormack, *Peacing Together,* op. cit. p 106.
7. Edwina Gateley, *I Hear a Seed Growing* (Anthony Clark, 1992) p 45.
8. David Augsburger, *Caring Enough to Not Forgive* (Herald Press, 1981) p 52.
9. Sue Ashdown, unpublished poem written in 1997.
10. The Hard Awakening, Bishop H. B. Dehqani-Tafti, Sohrab Books, Basingstoke, 1995.
11. Gerard Hughes, *God of Surprises* (London: DLT, 1985).